LEADING PEOPLE FOR THE FIRST TIME

A Practical Guide with Templates and Checklists
for New Managers and Team Leads

H. Maidre and H. Paas

CONTENTS

FOREWORD

When we first started writing this workbook, we knew one thing was certain: stepping into a leadership role, especially for the first time, is a wild mix of excitement, self-doubt, and straight-up confusion. It doesn't matter if you're in a scrappy startup, well-established company, school, or government office. Leading people for the first time is just hard. It is rewarding too, but that doesn't make it any less overwhelming.

The two of us wrote this together, by focusing on the topics where we each have the most experience. Between us, we've spent years working in startups, but we've also worked in very traditional companies, large corporations, multinational corporations and even with education. We are ideologically coming from a world where flexibility and fast decisions are the norm, but that doesn't mean this book is only useful for startup people. If anything, the core ideas like understanding yourself, communicating clearly, handling stress, and building trust - are relevant regardless where you work.

If you're in a place with plenty of rules, processes, and structure, this workbook might actually be even more useful. It's designed to make leadership feel more human: it's not the same as a book for how to manage people. And if your workplace is already pretty free-flowing, you'll find tools to help you bring a little more clarity and intention to all that freedom. Either way, we wrote this for everyone stepping into a leadership position for the first time, because the experience is similar for everyone.

If we can give you one piece of advice that will help you in your work and life journey no matter where it goes: it would be to find yourself a mentor. If we had had one earlier the process would have been faster and smoother from the get-go.

Our hope is that this book will give you space to pause, reflect, and grow into the kind of leader you actually want to be. We believe leadership is less about having all the answers and more about asking better questions, of yourself and of your team.

So welcome. No matter where you're leading, you're not alone. Let's figure this out together.

I'M THE BOSS, NOW WHAT?

Growing up, my mother used to tell me, "Being the boss at work must be great - you don't have to do the work; you just tell everyone else what to do!" It sounded appealing to a child, until I stepped into my first leadership role, where I realized how misleading my mothers words were.

My mother had seen my grandmother "the "boss lady" as an outsider looking in, and to her it seemed like all she did was delegate tasks to others, including her own children. But what outsiders often don't see is all the behind-the-scenes effort that leaders put in to keep everything running smoothly. They don't see the late nights, the tough decisions, or the constant juggling act to keep the team happy, productive, and aligned with the company's goals. My mother did not see that the tasks and chores expected of her were also preparing her for a future of independence and being her own boss. A good leader exposes their team to experiences and enables them to grow.

As a new leader, I faced the challenge of ensuring my team operated seamlessly, satisfying not just our objectives but also meeting the expectations of my own leaders. How could I make sure that our collective efforts were actually propelling the company forward?

That's where this workbook comes in. It's a compilation of the insights and tools, built over many years, that I wish I'd had when I first stepped into a leadership position. Over the years, through personal experiences, company training, and a deep dive into numerous management books, I've gathered a wealth of knowledge about effective leadership and coaching. The tools used to help new first time leaders in my own team find their feet and thrive.

The irony is that when I was just starting out, I had to prove myself before gaining access to the very trainings that would teach me how to excel in my role. Most resources are geared toward seasoned leaders looking to fine-tune their skills and make a bigger impact. But what about those of us just beginning our leadership journey? If I'd had access to these lessons earlier, I could have avoided many pitfalls and unnecessary "cleanup work" later on.

This workbook is designed for new leaders and meant to bridge that gap of growing into your new shoes. It provides you with practical advice and strategies from day one. Together, we'll explore how to lead effectively, support your team, impress your higher-ups, and contribute meaningfully to your organization's success.

Welcome to your leadership journey. Let's get started!

CHAPTER 1:
HOW TO SUCCEED IN YOUR NEW ROLE

Congrats! You've stepped into your first leadership role. This is an exciting moment marking the beginning of a journey filled with opportunities, challenges, and growth.

When I led my first team, I felt nervous. As I transitioned from a specialist who excelled individually to a leader responsible for guiding others my responsibilities and perspectives shifted in ways I hadn't expected. Leadership isn't merely about title, size of the team, or level of authority. It's fundamentally about inspiring, empowering, and influencing those around me to achieve shared goals. I wondered if I was doing a good job. I wanted my team to excel so we could give the company what it needed and help each person achieve more career growth.

I quickly realized that success required balancing both management (handling tasks like meeting targets and allocating resources) and leadership (motivating and guiding my team toward shared goals).

But it was hard without a clear roadmap of how to succeed. No one gave me a step-by-step guide. If leadership were that simple, anyone (or even an AI) could do it, but in reality, success isn't one-size-fits-all.

After doing the job for a while and then leading other leads - my goal was to have the leads that reported to me, know what success looks like. Having a clear idea of what is expected of one's work allows you to achieve it well. And remember that if no one has spelled out what success looks like, you have to ask. With that in mind, here's a streamlined guide to help you succeed as a new leader.

PART 1:
DEFINING SUCCESS FROM ALL ANGLES

YOUR OWN REFLECTION AND HOW YOU MEASURE YOURSELF AS A LEADER

Before diving into your daily responsibilities, pause to explore what leadership genuinely means to you. Reflect on the personal journey that brought you here, whether leadership was something you sought or an unexpected role thrust upon you. Both paths offer unique opportunities.

Ask yourself:

1. Why does this leadership role matter to me personally?
2. What sparked my interest in leading others, or how have circumstances led me here?
3. Think back to a time when you felt genuinely successful.
4. Was it after overcoming a challenging project?
5. Was it your idea that helped someone or something to succeed?
6. Perhaps when you saw your team or a team member flourish under your guidance?

As a leader, your personal sense of success often stems from:
- Achieving personal goals you have set for yourself
- Growing as a leader by noticing improvements in your skills and leadership abilities
- Seeing your team's performance change for the better
- Having a team that is content working under your leadership

How do you see yourself?

To take this reflection further, spend a few moments thinking about what leadership really means to **you**—beyond metrics and titles. This is about building your own leadership compass.

Grab a notebook or open a new document and write down three leadership goals you want to achieve in the next six months. If you prefer another timeline, we recommend anywhere from three months to a year—enough time to aim big, but still stay grounded.

Be bold and ambitious when making a long-term success plan. Your goal is to think big enough that you have something meaningful to strive for. Then, break it down into smaller, manageable steps so you'll have a realistic, actionable plan to measure progress. Use the help of this workbook, or even your lead or mentor, to shape your plan.

EXAMPLE GOALS FOR YOUR SUCCESS PLAN

"Master the art of delegation to empower my team."

"Foster an environment where open communication thrives."

"Lead my team to consistently exceed our project deadlines."

"Learn new skills to advance in my career like coaching, coding, Excel skills, etc."

"Stop new hires quitting after 6 months on the job."

Here are some additional questions you can explore to better understand your current mindset and where you want to grow:

Values & Meaning

- What kind of leader do I aspire to be—not just in skills, but in how I make others feel?
- What do I stand for as a leader?

What values do I want to consistently model for my team?

Strengths & Blind Spots

- What are the leadership strengths I naturally lean into?
- What feedback have I received in the past that stuck with me—for better or worse?
- Where do I tend to get stuck or second-guess myself?

Growth Mindset

- What's a recent challenge I've learned from in a leadership role?
- How do I respond when things don't go as planned?
- What am I curious to learn next?

THROUGH YOUR LEADER'S EYES AND HOW YOUR LEADER MEASURES YOU

Your lead plays a significant role in your journey. Just as it's your job to guide your team, it's your lead's job to guide you. Understanding what success looks like from their perspective is crucial. What do they measure? What metrics matter most to the company's success? How do they define their own success?

If these expectations aren't clearly communicated, take the initiative to ask. Your lead's perception of your success is often shaped by how well you align with these priorities and contribute to the bigger picture. As a lead of other leads I was positively impressed every time a newly minted leader came to ask me what success looks like through my eyes.

To better understand their expectations—and build a partnership grounded in trust and clarity—consider having a dedicated conversation to explore what success looks like through their lens.

Schedule a chat with your lead over a cup of coffee (virtual or real) and ask questions like:

Priority Alignment & Focus

- What are the top three priorities you'd like me to focus on right now?
- What challenges or goals are most important to our team this quarter?
- Are there any organizational shifts or changes I should keep in mind?

Success Metrics

- How will you measure my success in the first 90 days?
- What does long-term success look like in my role over the next 6–12 months?
- What indicators do you personally look for to know someone is doing well in a leadership role?

Expectations & Leadership Style

- What do you expect from me as a people leader?
- Are there aspects of my leadership style you'd like me to evolve or build on?
- What would a 'great job' look like from your point of view?

Feedback & Growth

- How do you prefer to give and receive feedback?
- What's the best way for me to check in with you on my progress?
- Where do you think I have the most potential to grow?

Team Dynamics & Support

- How do you think the team is doing overall, and how can I support their growth?
- Are there any specific areas where you'd like to see more consistency or change in the team's performance?
- What are the most important values you want me to uphold when leading this team?

THE TEAM'S PERSPECTIVE AND HOW YOUR TEAM MEASURES YOU

Your team is at the heart of your leadership role now. You can't do everything that's expected of you alone, and your success increasingly depends on your team's performance. They look to you for guidance, support, and inspiration.

As you grow in your role, it's important to get regular insight into how your leadership is being experienced by the people you lead. Listening deeply to their feedback not only helps them feel heard—it makes you a stronger, more adaptive leader.

After settling into your role, consider conducting an anonymous survey or having informal one-on-one chats to understand how you're doing in the areas that matter most to your team. Here are some example questions to ask:

Support and direction:

- When you're stuck or uncertain, how do you feel like you can reach out to me for help?
- In what kind of areas where you'd like more clarity or structure from me?
- How do I help remove obstacles or just add more to your plate?

Growth and development:

- How do you feel like you're growing professionally in your role?
- What can I do to support your learning or skill-building?
- How have I helped you find opportunities for advancement or stretch assignments?

Communication and feedback:

- How do you feel heard when you share ideas or concerns?
- How helpful and timely is the feedback you get from me?
- How do I create space for open, two-way conversations?

Team and culture morale:

- How would you describe the overall team atmosphere?
- What do I do that contributes positively to the culture—and what takes away from it?
- How included and valued do you feel on this team?

Vision and motivation:

- How do you understand how your work connects to our broader goals?
- How am I helping the team stay focused on what matters most?
- What inspires or motivates you about being on this team—and how can I support that?

Trust and accountability:

- How trusted do you feel to make decisions and own your work?
- How do you feel about the level of accountability on this team?
- How fairly and consistently do I address issues?

My leadership style:

- What's one thing I do as a leader that really works for you?
- What's one thing I could do differently to better support the team?
- If you were in my shoes, what would you try changing first?

This kind of feedback is invaluable. It helps you understand their needs, refine your approach, and build stronger connections.

CHECK IN ON A WEEKLY SCHEDULE WITH THE TEAM

Goals point you in the right direction, yet progress shows up in what you talk about every week. This helps you understand if you and your team are succeeding. A short, consistent check-in keeps the team aligned, surfaces problems early, and reminds everyone that their work matters. If you are taking over an existing team, likely this meeting is already in place and has a set agenda and way it is run. This may or may not be the best way to run it, it is simply the way it has always been done. I recommend thinking about what is the purpose of that meeting and making any changes to get it to fulfill that purpose. Here are some general guidelines for a weekly meeting that will help you think through if yours is serving the team's (and your) success or not.

How to set up a weekly check-in

1. Pick a regular day and time that works for most of the team and keep it unchanged so people can plan.
2. Limit the meeting to fifteen or thirty minutes to respect everyone's schedule. Stick to it.
3. Use a simple agenda: recent wins, current roadblocks, priorities for the coming week, and any help needed.
4. Invite each person to contribute, rotating who speaks first so quieter voices are heard. Close with clear next steps, note who owns what, and send a short recap.

Weekly time to get on the same page beats ad-hoc conversations. Regular face time reduces information gaps, lets you fix issues before they grow, and builds trust faster than occasional deep dives. Frequent feedback also helps you adjust your leadership style in real time and catch early signs of overload or disengagement.

Generally this is done on Mondays so people can get aligned on the plan for the rest of the week and you catch any issues before the team goes off executing in the wrong direction. Sometimes it is instead run on Fridays so everyone can learn from what happened in the past week. If client work does not allow for Monday or Friday meetings then it can be at whatever time of course. The key is keeping the time constant and making other work fit around it, because if it is an ad hoc meeting I can guarantee that it will get cancelled more often than not. You can learn more about how to run successful meetings, and how to waste as little time as necessary in pointless meetings, in Chapter 4.

These meetings do not need to be an hour long. It can just be 15 minutes. This depends on the size of your team and the nature of your work. But if you think it makes sense to have an hour or longer meeting once a month instead of 15 minutes every week - let me caution you. If there is something wrong and someone is working towards incorrect goals - would you want them to keep doing that for the next 3 weeks?

Remember - the goal is to help your team succeed. Check in meetings are to understand that they are heading to success and to remove any blockers in their way. Your team succeeding means you are succeeding.

Example:

One of your main priorities is to build strong connections and foster open communication. You decide on a goal: "By the end of the quarter, I will implement weekly team check-ins to enhance communication and address any concerns promptly."

Picture the following scenario: you notice team members completing tasks in isolation, rarely sharing updates or potential issues. Without regular touchpoints, you risk missing warning signs until problems become crises. By scheduling brief weekly meetings, however, you uncover issues earlier, delegate resources more wisely, and support team members who feel overwhelmed.

Situation	Without Weekly Check-ins	With Weekly Check-ins
Communication	People work in silos, unclear about shared objectives	Team openly exchanges ideas, staying aligned and motivated
Issue Resolution	Problems stay hidden and resurface when too late to fix	Concerns are flagged early and sorted before escalating
Team Morale	Employees feel disconnected, undervalued, or overlooked	Regular personal interactions boost trust, confidence, and social well-being
Accountability	Roles and responsibilities may be misunderstood	Clear assignments keep everyone on track, enhancing performance

By committing to brief, purposeful check-ins, you reinforce a culture of transparency and collaboration. These sessions become a forum for recognising achievements, clarifying priorities, and ensuring your team feels heard. Regular interactions also give you the chance to refine your leadership style in real time, helping you grow more confident and effective as a new leader.

THE BIGGER PICTURE AS IN HOW THE COMPANY MEASURES YOU

At an organizational level, your success contributes to the broader mission. The company likely measures your impact in ways that go beyond your individual performance—they're looking at how your work drives progress across teams, departments, and customer experiences.

You may be measured by:

- Key performance indicators (KPIs). Metrics tied to your role, such as revenue growth, project completion rates, or customer satisfaction scores
- Cultural impact. How you embody and promote the company's culture, values, and behaviors across the organization
- Strategic alignment. How your work connects to the company's big-picture goals and initiatives

It's your job as a leader to connect your team's work to these higher-level outcomes. That means being proactive about identifying which organizational metrics you can directly influence—and creating success plans that reflect those.

Schedule time to review your company's strategic goals, quarterly reports, or department OKRs (Objectives and Key Results), or whatever measures used where you work. Then ask your lead or senior peers:

- What business outcomes should I be focused on influencing this quarter?
- Which company metrics am I directly (or indirectly) accountable for?
- Once you've got clarity, write down 2–3 measurable goals aligned with the bigger picture.

Example company-aligned goals:

- Increase team productivity by 15% in the next quarter
- Enhance customer satisfaction scores through a new service protocol
- Reduce project completion timelines by 10% over the next six months
- Streamline internal workflows to cut admin time by 20%
- Increase employee engagement scores by 10% via targeted development
- Ensure 90% of the team completes professional training this quarter
- Launch a new cross-functional initiative within 90 days
- Identify and implement three automation tools to improve efficiency

Ask yourself:

- Which company or department KPIs can I realistically impact in my role?
- How does my team's work contribute to the overall strategy?
- Are there areas where I could drive more value or efficiency across the business?
- How do I make sure my team understands the connection between their goals and the company's goals?
- Am I a visible ambassador for the culture we're trying to build?

COMMON METRICS THAT DEFINE LEADERSHIP SUCCESS

Now that you've explored what success looks like through your own lens, as well as your team's, your lead's, and your company's—it's time to step back and look at the big picture.

While leadership can feel personal and team-specific, most organizations use a common set of metrics to evaluate leaders at any level. Whether or not your team interacts directly with customers, understanding these success factors helps you stay aligned and lead with purpose.

If your team is customer-facing, customer satisfaction and loyalty are essential. If your work is more internally focused, then innovation, efficiency, and collaboration will likely be in the spotlight. Either way, your ability to connect your team's work to larger goals is key. An easy way to think about this is to figure out who your customer is and how you're supposed to be serving them. Internally or externally your team has a purpose and that purpose is to meet some need - figure out what your purpose is and how to measure success in serving it.

Here are the most common metrics used to define leadership success. A lot of the success acronyms vary industry by industry so we've described the gist of what they mean. The acronym alphabet soup is below that. All the success measures and whatever systems to measure success fit into the below categories for what they are actually trying to achieve.

Team performance

- Meeting or exceeding goals, deadlines, and OKRs or KPIs
- Delivering high-quality, reliable results
- Reducing errors and improving over time

Engagement and morale

- Strong team satisfaction and low turnover
- Positive feedback from team members
- Participation in development and team-building initiatives

Communication and alignment

- Clear communication of goals and expectations
- Collaboration with other teams and stakeholders
- Helping your team understand how their work connects to the big picture

Operational excellence

- Smart use of budgets and resources
- Streamlined workflows and fewer bottlenecks
- Implementation of tools or processes that boost productivity

Customer impact

- Higher customer satisfaction and loyalty
- Positive reviews, referrals, or feedback
- Delivery of solutions that meet real customer needs

Growth and development

- Support for learning, upskilling, and career growth
- Encouragement of innovation and initiative
- Coaching team members to take on new challenges

Strategic contribution

- Work that supports long-term business objectives
- Proactive risk management and problem-solving
- Leading or contributing to initiatives that improve resilience and adaptability

You will probably start hearing a lot more acronyms now that you are in charge of people and their results. It will sound like alphabet soup at first, I personally just sat in meetings with a tab open to web search, to quickly what the acronyms people were talking about meant.

If your company is serious about getting new leadership up to speed they will have some page explaining what all the acronyms important to business mean. Read that before any big meetings and planning sessions. Ask your own lead what are the most important metrics for your team to move. Ask what your success is measured by.

If your workplace has no such list: find the yearly or quarterly plans and business results. These will be full of acronyms. Search or ask an AI for explanations with reference links. Knowing what everyone else is referring to and using them in conversation puts you ahead of the game faster.

Here is a list of commonly used success measure acronyms and their meanings:

KPI – Key Performance Indicator. A specific, trackable measure such as on-time delivery, error rate, or revenue per employee that shows whether a goal is being met and where effort needs to shift.

OKR – Objectives and Key Results. A goal-setting framework that pairs a clear objective like "Launch new client portal" with a few measurable results such as "95 % uptime, 1 000 monthly active users, break-even in six months" so progress stays visible.

ROI – Return on Investment. The percentage you earn or lose after subtracting the cost of the investment from the gain, used to judge whether money, time, or people have been well spent.

NPS – Net Promoter Score. A quick customer-loyalty gauge that asks, "How likely are you to recommend us?" Scores range from -100 to +100; the higher the number, the more promoters you have.

CSAT – Customer Satisfaction Score. A post-interaction rating, often 1–5, that shows how happy customers are with a product, service, or support call and helps teams spot service gaps early.

CAC – Customer Acquisition Cost. The total sales and marketing spend needed to win a new customer, most useful when compared with lifetime value.

CLV (or LTV) – Customer Lifetime Value. The net revenue you expect from one customer over the entire relationship; sustainable growth relies on keeping CLV much higher than CAC.

MRR – Monthly Recurring Revenue. Predictable subscription income booked each month, essential for cash-flow planning in SaaS or membership models.

ARR – Annual Recurring Revenue. The twelve-month version of MRR that shows long-term revenue stability.

Churn Rate –The percentage of customers or revenue you lose in a given period; keeping churn low protects the growth you have already paid for.

ARPU – Average Revenue per User. The mean amount a single customer brings in during a set time frame, handy for seeing whether upgrades or price changes are working.

EBITDA – Earnings Before Interest, Taxes, Depreciation, and Amortization. A proxy for operating profit that strips out financing and accounting choices so you can compare core performance across companies.

Gross Margin –The percentage left after subtracting the direct cost of making or delivering your product, showing how efficiently the business turns sales into usable cash.

eNPS – Employee Net Promoter Score. An internal pulse that mirrors NPS but asks staff how likely they are to recommend the company as a workplace; rising scores often track with better retention and engagement.

Ask yourself:

1. Which of these metrics are most relevant to your role right now?
2. Which ones do you want to improve or focus on more in the next quarter?

PART 2:
BUILDING YOUR PERSONAL LEADERSHIP BLUEPRINT

Now that you've explored what success looks like from different angles, it's time to define what success looks like to *you*. This section will help you craft your own leadership blueprint—clarifying who you want to be, what you want to achieve, and how you'll handle the ups and downs of leading a team.

DEFINE YOUR LEADERSHIP VISION

Step 1: Identify effective leadership qualities

Think of leaders you admire—personal acquaintances, public figures, or professional mentors. List five specific qualities or behaviors that made them impactful (for example: empathy, decisiveness, innovation).

Step 2: Connect qualities to your values

Reflect on how these qualities align with your personal values. Identify core values that you want to embody consistently in your leadership style.

Step 3: Visualize your leadership vision

Clearly envision the leader you aspire to become. How do you demonstrate these qualities and values daily? This vision is your leadership compass. Return to it often as your role evolves.

Ask yourself:

- What kind of leader do I aspire to be?
- In six months, how do I want my team and manager to describe me?

Maybe you see yourself as an innovative leader who fosters creativity, or perhaps a compassionate leader who champions team well-being. Defining this vision sets the compass for your journey and helps you become leader you aspire to be and your team needs.

TRACK AND CELEBRATE YOUR PROGRESS

Celebrating progress is more than a feel-good ritual; it cements new neural pathways that say, "I can do hard things." When you pause to notice a small win, such as closing a tricky ticket or calming a tense meeting, you turn an abstract goal into evidence that growth is happening. That self-recognition fuels motivation far better than external praise alone.

Ritualizing celebration also teaches your team what good looks like. A quick "Here's what went well and why" turns success into a repeatable pattern. Even setbacks become easier to bounce back from because yesterday's win reminds you that progress is rarely linear yet always possible.

How you log these moments matters less than why. Jot a few sentences in a notebook, drop a voice memo on your phone, or add a quick line to a running doc. The point is to capture enough detail so future you can relive the feeling and extract the lesson. Some leaders pick one weekly highlight and share it during check-in meetings to model reflective practice; others set a calendar invite titled "Celebrate" to create a five-minute pause. Pick whatever rhythm keeps you consistent.

Celebrating your wins is a direct antidote to imposter syndrome because each acknowledgment replaces vague self-doubt with concrete evidence of competence. By pausing to mark a finished project, a positive client email, or even a well-run meeting, you create a growing archive of proof that you belong in the role. Over time these small moments stack up, training your mind to recall successes as readily as it recalls missteps. That balanced memory makes it easier to challenge the inner narrative of "I just got lucky" and, instead, to view progress as the natural result of skill and effort.

You should also consider keeping a "bragdoc." A brag document is a living list of your achievements, impact stories, and positive feedback. The name sounds tongue-in-cheek, but the practice is serious self-care. When imposter syndrome whispers that you are falling short, flipping through concrete evidence of past wins offers a fast reality check. Over time the document becomes an internal résumé, making annual reviews or salary negotiations less stressful because the facts are already collected, quantified, and ready to share. Leaders who keep a bragdoc find they talk about their work with more clarity and confidence. These skills pay dividends whether you are requesting a raise or championing your team's success.

HANDLING SETBACKS AND FAILURES

Setbacks are inevitable in leadership—and they're not just obstacles, they're opportunities. How you respond to them plays a big role in shaping your growth, resilience, and leadership maturity. Rather than viewing mistakes as roadblocks, see them as valuable learning moments that help you refine your approach, strengthen your team, and become more confident in navigating future challenges. Here's how to face them with confidence.

Step 1: Reframe failure as a learning opportunity

Reflect on setbacks with curiosity rather than self-criticism. Ask yourself:

- What went wrong, and why?
- What could I do differently next time?
- What lessons can I share with my team?

Step 2: Address team mistakes constructively

When your team faces failure, focus on solutions rather than blame. Encourage open discussions where employees feel safe owning up to mistakes. This builds trust and continuous improvement.

If you feel really bad about a setback right now - you will find more help in Chapter 8 about tough moments, especially the second part on post-mortems. This too shall pass, you will be stronger after, take it one day at a time and you will bounce back.

PART 3:
STRENGTHENING YOUR
HABITS AND PRACTICES

As a leader, your growth isn't just about big breakthroughs—it's about the small, intentional habits you build every day. These practices keep you grounded, focused, and continuously improving. Think of them as leadership rituals that help you reflect, adjust, and stay aligned with your goals.

EXERCISES TO ELEVATE YOUR LEADERSHIP

1. THE WEEKLY SUCCESS SNAPSHOT

Take 15 minutes at the end of each week to reflect on your progress. This simple routine builds awareness and momentum over time. This is really important for you to keep to, it seems like an easy way to gain a time slot to have a meeting with someone else when asked. But keep this time for yourself, you need to continually take a moment to evaluate your progress and direction. Make it a non-negotiable habit. More on how to guard your calendar in Chapter 4.

Ask yourself:

1. What went well this week? What contributed to those wins?
2. What challenges did I face? How did I respond, and what did I learn?
3. What feedback did I receive (direct or indirect)? How can I apply it?

This structured reflection keeps your attention on growth and helps you spot gaps that need work before they become bigger issues.

2. ESTABLISH A FEEDBACK LOOP

Ongoing feedback is essential for effective leadership. Create a loop that includes perspectives from multiple sources:

- From your lead – hopefully your lead has scheduled brief check-ins to review your performance and alignment. If not ask for feedback regularly.
- From your team – encourage open conversations, or if needed, use anonymous surveys to gather honest insights.
- From peers – after cross-functional projects or collaborations, ask for feedback on your leadership style and communication.

A note on anonymity. While anonymous feedback can encourage honesty, it sometimes lacks nuance or context. A good balance is to involve a neutral facilitator (like your manager or HR) who can help gather insights constructively. This approach protects professionalism and encourages candor without creating defensiveness.

The key is to create a culture where feedback is normalized—not feared. It's one of the fastest ways to grow. Feedback is a gift—it offers insights you might not see on your own.

3. CREATE A LEADERSHIP SUCCESS BOARD

A visual board keeps your goals top of mind and celebrates progress in real time. Place it somewhere you'll see regularly, whether physical or digital.

Include:

- Display key metrics: keep your KPIs front and center.
- Highlight goals: post your SMART (see Chapter 2) goals where you can see them daily.
- Celebrate wins: pin up notes, emails, or tokens of appreciation you've received.

This board isn't just motivational—it's a living reflection of your growth and impact as a leader. Return to it often to stay focused and inspired.

PART 4:
LEADING THROUGH CHANGE

PRACTICAL STRATEGIES TO THRIVE IN YOUR NEW ROLE – GROWTH, SETBACKS, AND NEW DYNAMICS

Adjust your leadership style. Know about different classical leadership styles as an example: coercive, authoritative, pacesetting, democratic, affiliative, coaching - and experiment to see what best supports your team. Your style may need to shift based on the people or situation. Stay flexible and responsive.

Balance control with acceptance. Focus your energy on what you can directly influence—like daily processes and team development. For everything else, practice acceptance and adaptability. This models emotional resilience for your team.

Build your influence. Move from doing the work yourself to guiding others. Influence comes from clear communication, consistent actions, and motivation tailored to each person on your team. We already talked about the importance of taking the time to check in with yourself about your own progress. You can do that on a different schedule for small things and big things. Weekly you keep track of how the small steps are going, but occasionally you need to take a bigger picture view. Here are some ways to do that.

Check-ins with yourself

Take a few minutes each week to ask:

- Am I moving closer to my objectives?
- Do I need to adjust my approach?

Adapting to evolving demands is a core trait of capable leaders. A rigid plan rarely withstands the unexpected twists of real-world challenges, so allow yourself to adjust and improve continually.

Monthly success review:

- Reflect on your impact: What's working well? Where can you improve?
- Document achievements: Keep a record of milestones and lessons learned.
- Communicate progress: Share updates with your lead to stay aligned.

Celebrate milestones, don't wait for the big victories to celebrate:

- Team achievements: recognize collective efforts and successes.
- Personal growth: maybe you handled a difficult situation better than before—that's worth celebrating!

Celebrations boost morale and motivate everyone to keep pushing forward. It can be anything from shoutouts during a meeting, a simple group email, a short group huddle to celebratory dinners and days off. It all depends on your organisation and budget.

Remember, a small gesture is always better than nothing.

Ask yourself:

1. What actions can I take this week to align my performance with my team's and organization's goals?
2. How can I support my team in achieving their best?
3. What small or significant actions can I take to create an environment where my team can do their best work?

EMBRACING THE LEADERSHIP MINDSET

Shifting from specialist to leader is transformative, requiring you to manage broader responsibilities and greater ambiguity. Instead of controlling every detail, focus on influencing through inspiration, clarity, and empowerment. Balance immediate tasks with strategic, long-term goals, always prioritizing your team's growth and morale.

Leadership is not about seeking perfection but about learning, evolving, and making a tangible difference. The route to success is lined with both setbacks and breakthroughs, each shaping you into the leader you aim to become. Stay open to feedback, keep a clear focus on your goals, and continually adapt to new challenges. In doing so, you will do more than simply meet expectations—you will surpass them.

Embrace the learning curve, remain open-minded, and celebrate each milestone on this rewarding journey. Remember, great leadership isn't about having all the answers but creating an environment where collaboration, innovation, and collective excellence flourish. Your journey from specialist to leader offers an exceptional opportunity for lasting impact—on your team's success and your personal growth.

WHAT IF YOU TRANSITION FROM A PEER TO A LEAD?

Transitioning from peer to team lead can feel like crossing a delicate line. One moment you're talking about weekend plans; the next, you're assigning tasks and offering critiques. You might worry about being too relaxed or too tough, especially if you were close with your teammates. I remember feeling a wave of nervousness when I first ran a meeting with people who had been my peers. Being direct about the shift and explaining what I wanted to achieve as a leader helped establish respect without losing that friendly connection.

When you hold your first team meeting, try being open about how your role has changed. Share your top priorities, like fairness, clarity, and honest communication. Let people know some boundaries will shift: you won't share certain details the way you once did, but you're still you. If resentment or competition is brewing, tackle it before it grows. Offer private chats to anyone feeling sidelined, and remind everyone you value their skills and want them to succeed. If you were in direct competition with someone that you now lead and they got passed over - you need to address that directly. Things will stay festering if you do not have a conversation about it. You are the lead now - act like it.

Once you settle in, watch for lingering team habits. Some folks may assume you'll judge them based on past knowledge. Instead, set consistent performance standards for everyone, showing you prize fairness above bias. Over time, a balanced approach—firm yet willing to listen—helps preserve camaraderie. Being liked is good, but genuine respect for your integrity and guidance benefits everyone more in the long run.

It also helps to talk with each team member early. I recall pulling aside a friend who became my direct report to say, "I still value our friendship, but my responsibilities have changed, and I want us to succeed together." That short, candid chat eased the tension and established healthy boundaries. Scheduling these one-on-one conversations shows you aren't suddenly aloof, yet you're serious about your new duties.

Bringing clarity to expectations right away can smooth the path. If you once shared deadlines casually, now's the time to formalize them so everyone sees you're acting fairly. If someone feels upset about your promotion, keep your door open. I once faced a former teammate who resented my new title, and our talk started with tension. Naming the issue—"I sense you're frustrated; how can we fix this?"—led to respect on both sides. Confronting concerns head-on and setting transparent standards prove your commitment to the team remains solid, even with your new authority.

It can feel odd to suddenly oversee people who once shared your daily gripes. A friend of mine assumed we'd keep venting about work like before, but I had to say, "I'm still here to listen, but I can't rant the way I used to." Though awkward at first, that frank conversation helped us redefine our relationship without losing our bond.

Another practical move is to limit casual social events at the start. You don't have to cut them out entirely, but a bit of distance highlights that things have changed. If you do go out as a group, keep it friendly while remaining professional about work topics. People will adapt and respect your new role, and soon you'll find a better balance between old friendships and new leadership obligations. My leader who was supporting me when I was just starting out recommended to me to avoid alcohol at company parties after I became a lead in charge of others. To be there more to support people and keep a cool head in case I need it. Now it creates trust to not be there checking up on people, you need to create an atmosphere where people feel comfortable, but as a lead you can't afford to get blackout drunk, have a drink or two but keep yourself respectable. Because you are in a role that demands respect, so you should demand respectability from yourself.

Now back to the situation of coming ahead of someone who used to be your peer. If a teammate is upset they didn't get the promotion, address that tension before it festers. Maybe invite them to talk privately: "I know this might be disappointing. I'd love to hear how we can still collaborate well." Simply acknowledging their feelings, instead of brushing them off, can be a relief for someone who feels overlooked. If you are in a large company where opportunities abound - commit to helping the person now on your team succeed and get a promotion in the next possible spot. In case you are in a hard situation where the person trying to get prompted lacks all needed leadership qualities, you need to start gently guiding them toward other ways of growing their career that do not include being in charge of other people.

I've found that a small gesture of respect—like highlighting someone's strengths or asking for their input—can shift rivalry to collaboration. If resentment lingers, keep it professional and focus on shared goals. You can't force a friendship, but consistent expectations and genuine openness tend to ease hard feelings over time.

Calling out a former pal when their work slips can feel daunting, but you can focus on the future instead of past mistakes. Maybe say, "I need you to step up on these tasks, and I'm here to help if you're stuck." It shows firmness with genuine care, reminding them you want everyone to do their best rather than simply handing out criticism.

For someone who was known to slack, specific goals and deadlines can work wonders. Once, I helped a struggling teammate by creating a basic improvement plan with measurable targets and regular check-ins. Seeing my support and the clear structure eased their negativity. Transparent expectations show you're serious about performance but also committed to fairness.

It's normal to want old teammates to keep seeing you as the approachable friend. You might feel tempted to maintain every friendship as it was, but deep down, you know you have to make difficult calls. Early on, I tried keeping things casual so nobody would think I'd turned into a stiff manager. Each time I bent a rule to stay on everyone's good side, though, the team ultimately suffered. Eventually, I realized letting things slide helped no one, including the friends counting on my leadership.

Remember, fairness doesn't mean being cold. You can show empathy while still being clear about expectations. If a friend is often late, treat it the same way you would with anyone else, blending compassion and accountability. I once learned a teammate's tardiness was tied to childcare issues, so we adjusted her schedule to meet both family and work demands. That flexibility proved we could solve real-life problems without lowering standards.

Over time, people come to respect a leader who's consistent and holds everyone to the same bar. They may not applaud every single decision, but they'll trust you're looking out for the team's long-term success. Show that your new boundaries aren't about flexing power but about raising expectations for everyone, including yourself. When folks see you're willing to put in the effort and own your responsibilities, they'll value you as both a leader and a person. You don't have to be best friends with everyone, but you can blend respect, empathy, and consistency in your leadership. Once that becomes clear, you'll keep plenty of genuine camaraderie, and the team will appreciate you for the right reasons.

CHECKLIST:
PEER-TO-LEADER RESET

Use this after your promotion to ensure you're leading clearly and fairly:

- [ ] I've communicated my goals and new responsibilities to the team

- [ ] I've set clear expectations that apply to everyone equally

- [ ] I've had 1:1s with former peers to reset dynamics

- [ ] I've addressed any noticeable tension early and openly

- [ ] I'm learning to balance approachability with fairness and structure

- [ ] I'm letting go of needing to be "liked" to focus on being "trusted"

- [ ] I have a vision of who I am as a lead.

CHAPTER 2:
MASTERING PRODUCTIVITY AS A NEW LEADER

PRODUCTIVITY: A LEADERSHIP LENS

As a new leader, your relationship with productivity changes. It's no longer about checking off every item on a to-do list. It's about using your time and energy with intention, aligning efforts to what matters most, and building systems that support your team's success.

In this chapter, you'll learn how to:

- Prioritize effectively using simple frameworks
- Delegate with confidence using the 70% rule
- Plan your week for clarity and focus
- Use powerful tools to manage tasks and lead strategically
- Leverage tech tools that simplify and scale your work

Feeling overwhelmed is common. When you step into leadership, the to-do list grows—but your time doesn't. This chapter will help you:

- Shift from doing it all to doing what matters
- Design systems that reduce mental clutter
- Focus on leadership priorities, not reactive work

For support on managing mental overload, see Chapter 9 on mental well-being.

This chapter mainly focuses on a variety of tools to get your productivity to a better place. A lot of the tools are similar to each other. Try them out to see which one suits your situation and style best.

PART 1:
CORE PRODUCTIVITY TOOLS
FOR PRIORITIZATION

EISENHOWER MATRIX

Also known as the Urgent-Important Matrix, this tool categorizes tasks into four quadrants:

Imagine having a clear roadmap that helps you decide what to tackle first and what can wait. The Eisenhower Matrix offers just that by categorizing your tasks based on their urgency and importance. Picture your to-do list divided into four quadrants:

1. Urgent and important: these are the tasks that require immediate attention. Think of them as crises or deadlines that cannot be postponed. For instance, addressing a critical client issue or meeting an imminent project deadline falls into this category. Handling these tasks right away ensures that you maintain control over pressing matters.

2. Important but not urgent: these tasks are essential for long-term success but don't demand immediate action. Examples include strategic planning, personal development, or building relationships within your team. Scheduling time for these activities helps you stay focused on your overarching goals without the constant pressure of deadlines.

3. Urgent but not important: these tasks might seem pressing but don't significantly contribute to your primary objectives. Delegating these to team members can free up your time for more impactful work. For example, routine administrative tasks or responding to non-critical emails can be effectively handled by others.

4. Neither urgent nor important: these are low-value activities that can often be eliminated to save time. Activities like excessive social media browsing or attending irrelevant meetings fall into this category. Cutting these out allows

you to concentrate on what truly matters.

By consistently applying the Eisenhower Matrix, you prevent reactive behavior and ensure that you're dedicating your energy to tasks that drive meaningful progress.

Eisenhower Matrix helps you focus on strategic thinking. You often make your greatest contributions in the "important but not urgent" quadrant. These tasks may not demand your attention right away, but they matter for your long-term success. By prioritizing them, you steer clear of getting trapped in a reactive cycle.

When you delegate tasks that are "urgent but not important," you lighten your mental load and avoid overwhelm and possible burnout. This also empowers your team and frees you to concentrate on leadership priorities.

By cutting out tasks that are "neither urgent nor important," you eliminate distractions and open up more time for meaningful work. Following this principle makes it easier to see which demands you can confidently turn down.

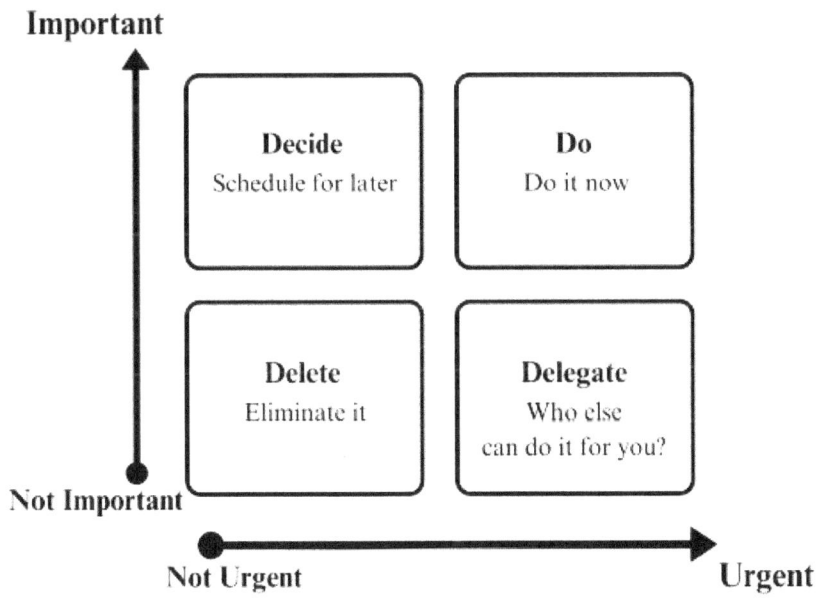

Take 10-15 minutes and empty your head of your ongoing tasks.

First off:

- List your tasks.
- Categorize: place each task into the appropriate quadrant.
- Act accordingly
  - o Do Now: tackle urgent and important tasks immediately.
  - o Schedule: allocate time for important but not urgent tasks.
  - o Delegate: assign urgent but not important tasks to team members.
  - o Eliminate: remove tasks that don't add value.

Then pair the Eisenhower Matrix with time blocking to structure your day. For example:

- Morning: 30 minutes for email triage and prioritizing tasks.
- Midday: 2 hours for deep work on strategic projects.
- Afternoon: 1 hour for team check-ins or resolving operational issues.

As a bonus question to go deeper - ask yourself:

- "What leadership activities am I neglecting, and how can I prioritize them this week?"
- "Am I spending too much time on tasks that others could handle?"

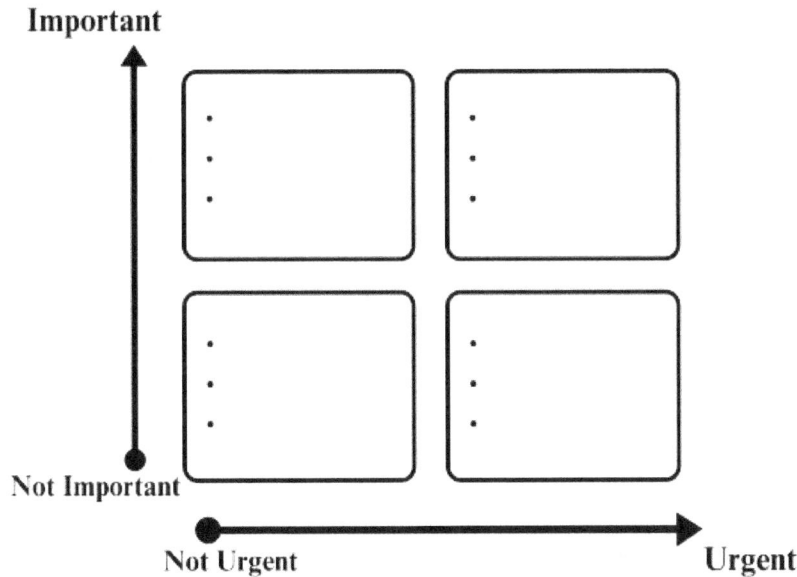

Important

Not Important

Not Urgent

Urgent

THE PARETO PRINCIPLE

The Pareto principle, known as the 80/20 rule, offers a potent way to boost productivity by zeroing in on the tasks that bring the biggest impact. As a leader, you're faced with countless responsibilities, but not all of them contribute equally to success. The Pareto principle helps you identify the 20% of tasks that generate 80% of the outcomes, letting you channel your energy where it really matters. The principle is often attributed to Vilfredo Pareto, an Italian economist who observed that about 80% of Italy's wealth was held by roughly 20% of its population. Over time, people noticed that this 80/20 rule shows up in many areas—from business and productivity to personal development—illustrating how a small fraction of efforts often produces the largest results.

Here's how you can apply the Pareto principle in your work. Start by identifying high-impact activities. Take stock of your tasks and projects, and ask which ones directly drive your team's success or your leadership goals. These might be strategic planning, mentoring, or eliminating a key bottleneck in a critical project. Next, reallocate your time so you devote more energy to that crucial 20%, and see if there's a way to delegate or cut down on the remaining 80%. Finally, reflect and refine regularly, because your top 20% can change as priorities shift. It helps to schedule weekly or monthly check-ins just to ensure you're still pouring your energy into what truly matters.

As a new leader it may seem like everything is important and you just need more time instead of deprioritizing. So here are a few examples of where your impact can be best spent.

High-impact tasks: planning a team strategy session, coaching a team member to resolve a recurring issue, creating a proposal for a high-visibility project.

Low-impact tasks: attending a meeting without a clear agenda, responding to every email immediately, manually compiling data that could be automated.

This is similar to the Eisenhower Matrix: you are separating the important from the unimportant. 80/20 helps you set your focus and figure out what gets you the most impact. As a leader the Eisenhower Matrix is good at reminding you to also delegate tasks and delete them. With 80/20 it is implied that what is unimportant needs to get off your plate.

EXERCISE: APPLYING THE 80/20 RULE

1. List your tasks and responsibilities.
   Write down all the tasks you've handled in the past week or anticipate for the upcoming week.

2. Categorize by impact.
   Divide them into two categories:
   - High-impact tasks: these directly drive results, align with your team's goals, or support your leadership development.
   - Low-impact tasks: may feel urgent but have little effect on long-term success.

3. Analyze your time allocation.

   Write down the amount of time spent on each task. Is the majority of your time going to high-impact activities?

   There are also many tools that you can add to your computer or browser that automatically track what sites you visit or apps you use - this may give you an easy look into where your time is going.

4. Reallocate and plan.

   Adjust your schedule to prioritize high-impact tasks. For example:

   - Block time for strategic projects or one-on-one mentoring.
   - Batch or delegate routine administrative work.
   - Say no to low-value meetings.

5. Set a goal for improvement.

   Commit to shifting at least 10-20% of your time from low-impact to high-impact activities in the coming week. Track the results and refine as needed.

These 2 prioritisation guides are your foundation. As a lead you need to learn to focus on what is most important and how to trust your team and get them to pull their weight. When both of those parts work you can maximise the impact you and your team have on bringing home the results, each in their own way where you can have maximum impact.

PART 2:
LEADERSHIP ACTIONS

DELEGATION - YOUR SECRET WEAPON

Shifting from doing everything yourself to empowering others is a huge challenge for new leaders. As an individual contributor, you probably shone by completing tasks quickly and controlling each outcome. Yet as a leader, clinging to that approach can undermine your productivity and your team's growth.

Many new leaders hesitate to delegate because they fear losing control; trusting others with tasks they can handle feels risky. They may also believe no one else can execute the work to the same standard and worry that assigning extra responsibilities will overload their team.

These fears are natural but counterproductive. Leadership is about achieving results through others. Holding onto tasks deprives your team of growth opportunities and yourself of time for strategic focus.

To delegate effectively you first need to identify the tasks to delegate. Pinpoint tasks that don't require your unique expertise, could help your team members grow, or eat up time you should be spending on higher-level leadership work. By handing these off, you free yourself to focus on strategic priorities and big-picture decisions.

Next you match tasks to the right people. Assign responsibilities based on each person's skills, interests, and experience. Aim to align tasks with their professional development goals, so they gain valuable hands-on learning while moving the team's progress forward.

As an example, you can assign a team member who usually prefers structure to lead a small project, offering guidance as needed so they build confidence in less-structured situations. Alternatively you can give a team member who enjoys autonomy a detailed task to help them develop attention to detail while still allowing room for creative problem-solving. Now if someone on your team is a big-picture visionary, ask them to lead a brainstorming session or shape the strategic direction for a project. Pair them with a more detail-oriented colleague to handle scheduling and follow-up, ensuring they can focus on what they do best.

Make sure to provide clear instructions. Spell out your expectations, timeline, and the resources they'll need. Describe what a successful result looks like, so everyone is clear on the outcomes you want. State clearly what level of freedom they have and what you are expecting, i.e. do you want them to research and come back to you to make a decision together, are you expecting recommendations, do you want them to take action and get something done? Make that clear and ask them to reflect back to you what they understood the task is. Read more about how to reflect and other coaching techniques in Chapter 6.

Support your team through it all. Once you delegate, allow your team to take ownership of their tasks. Steer clear of micromanaging, but stay available if they have questions or need guidance. This blend of trust and accessibility builds confidence and accountability.

The 70% Rule, as articulated by Jim Schleckser in Great CEOs Are Lazy, emphasizes the power of delegation in leadership. Schleckser advises that if someone can execute a task at least 70% as well as you can, it should be delegated. This not only frees up your time for higher-level responsibilities but also serves as a valuable coaching opportunity for your team. If no one on your team meets this threshold, your top priority must shift to training and development. As a leader, your role is no longer to be the specialist but to cultivate and empower those around you.

Here are some ways to say it out loud. If you have little experience delegating it may seem odd to you to start, but when you think about it a little more you have been delegating and been delegated to in all aspects of your life. It's just not called delegation in conversation. See the following examples and what you recognise from life. Note that there are important distinctions in how to delegate well, by asking it right. Instead of asking a yes or no question like "do" you have questions you need to ask "what" questions they have. This leads to actual understanding by both parties. Again there is more info in Chapter 6 on coaching questions.

- Assigning the task: "I believe you're the right person for this project because of your skills in [area]."
- Clarifying expectations: "Here's what I'm looking for by [deadline]: [specific deliverable]. What questions do you have?"
- Offering support: "I'm here if you need resources or run into roadblocks."
- Building confidence: "I trust your expertise. I'm excited to see your approach."

EXERCISE: MATCHING TASKS TO TEAM MEMBERS/DELEGATING TASKS

1. List your team's key tasks. Write down the main responsibilities and projects your team handles.
2. Assess each task. Determine whether each task requires autonomy and problem-solving, or structure and clarity.
3. Assign tasks mindfully
   - Autonomous tasks: assign to those who thrive on taking initiative and enjoy finding creative solutions.
   - Structured tasks: assign to those who prefer clear guidelines and excel when expectations are well-defined.
4. Encourage the team's growth. Challenge team members to step outside their comfort zones gradually. Support them with coaching (see Chapter 7) and feedback.
5. Leverage their strengths. Whenever possible, give tasks that align with each person's natural talents. This boosts motivation, engagement, and results.

There are 2 tables in the next pages, the first filled with potential examples and next an empty one for you to fill in with your own team and tasks.

1 Task	2 Autonomy/ Structure	3 Team Member
[Task Name]	Autonomy/ Structure	[Team Member Name]
Develop Marketing Strategy	Autonomy	Alex
Update Compliance Checklist	Structure	Jamie
Lead Team Brainstorming Session	Autonomy	Casey
Schedule & Track Deliverables	Structure	Taylor

4 Reason for Assignment	5 Growth Opportunity/Strength Utilization	6 Support Plan
Why this team member is suited for this task (e.g., aligns with their talents, builds new skills, supports team objectives).	Describe how this assignment challenges their weaknesses or leverages their strengths (e.g., encourage initiative, focus on attention to detail).	Outline coaching, feedback, or resources provided to help them succeed (e.g., regular check-ins, templates, pairing with a mentor).
Alex thrives in creative and strategic roles and enjoys big-picture thinking.	Strength: Leverage Alex's visionary skills to shape strategic direction.	Pair Alex with a detail-oriented teammate for scheduling and execution.
Jamie excels in tasks with clear guidelines and has experience in regulatory work.	Growth: Help Jamie build confidence in presenting updates to leadership.	Provide a checklist template and conduct weekly check-ins.
Casey is known for generating creative ideas and inspiring collaboration among peers.	Strength: Utilize Casey's collaborative energy to foster team innovation.	Offer tips on managing group dynamics and ensure clear objectives for the session.
Taylor is highly organized and detail-oriented, making them ideal for ensuring deadlines are met.	Growth: Encourage Taylor to take ownership of project status reporting to boost visibility with leadership.	Provide a project management tool and templates for tracking deliverables.

1 Task	2 Autonomy/Structure	3 Team Member

4 Reason for Assignment	5 Growth Opportunity/Strength Utilization	6 Support Plan

PLANNING WITH PURPOSE

As a leader, your most valuable asset isn't your to-do list - it's your time. How you plan your week directly shapes your impact, your clarity, and your ability to lead intentionally. Results come from planning, stop just reacting. You will see more impact and success if you plan ahead so you can work toward the goals that you want to achieve instead of just reacting to what other people throw on your plate.

You don't create change by rushing through endless tasks. You create it by building habits - and one of the most powerful habits you can form is weekly planning. Think of it as a personal strategy session: a quiet moment to pause, zoom out, and decide what matters most in the days ahead.

Weekly planning goes beyond simply listing tasks. It gives the week a clear sense of direction, helps you sort outcomes by real importance, and keeps you rooted in the work that genuinely pushes your team and its goals ahead.

Without a plan, it's easy to slip into reactive mode: putting out fires, jumping between requests, and losing sight of long-term objectives. With a plan, you take the wheel. You lead with intention, not just urgency.

Here's a structure to help you plan your week like a leader. Not just a doer.

1. Set Your Top 3 Outcomes

   Decide on the three most meaningful things you want to achieve this week. These should be high-impact, forward-moving outcomes, not just routine tasks. Ask yourself:

   - What matters most this week?
   - What moves the needle for my team or projects?

2. Review and Delegate

   Look at everything on your plate. Then, ask:

   - What must I personally do?
   - What can I delegate to empower someone else?

   Delegation isn't about offloading, it's about building capacity and trust across your team.

3. Block Your Time Intentionally

   Use time blocking to schedule focused sessions for deep work, team check-ins, and planning. Protect these blocks. That means treating them like real meetings: with yourself.

4. Practice the Power of "No"

   Decide which tasks don't belong on your list, either this week or ever. If it's not aligned, not urgent, or not meaningful, remove it. Archive it. Say no with intention so you can say yes to what matters.

5. Reflect and Refine at the End of the Week

   Book 15 minutes on Friday (or whenever your week wraps) to reflect, by yourself.

   - What worked well?
   - What could improve?
   - What small win deserves to be celebrated?

Reflection builds momentum. It helps you grow into a more adaptive, intentional leader with every week that passes. You need to actually book time for yourself to do that and then keep that time. See again chapter 4 on how to keep your calendar safe from too many meetings.

Schedule a 30-minute planning session each Monday (or Friday afternoon if that's your reset point). Create a recurring calendar block. Make it a sacred time. Just for you, your brain, and your big-picture goals.

Before Monday starts, ask yourself:

- What are my 3 most impactful goals this week?
- What should I delegate or eliminate?
- Have I blocked time for focused work and team check-ins?
- Which habit do I want to try or strengthen?

What can I say "no" to that doesn't align?

TOP 5 TIME MANAGEMENT TIPS FOR TAKEAWAY

1. Prioritize with the Eisenhower Matrix - focus on high-impact tasks; delegate or eliminate lower-value ones.
2. Start each day with a plan - spend a few minutes reviewing priorities to stay aligned with weekly goals.
3. Time blocking - schedule specific times for focused work and protect them from interruptions.
4. Set availability boundaries -limit time spent on emails and ad-hoc requests by scheduling dedicated periods. Set up an Out of Office auto-reply that lets people know your reply times and rules. (See Chapter 4)
5. Batch similar tasks - group tasks like time for email replies or meetings to improve efficiency.

PART 3:
MORE TOOLS FOR PRIORITIZATION

Earlier in the chapter we covered a few of the most impactful tools, like the Eisenhower Matrix and the Pareto Principle. But since we're all different, these methods might not always suit our personal style or leadership approach. That's why we're introducing a few more useful resources for you to explore. Try them out and see which one is the best for you to go forward with.

PROGRESS TRACKING TEMPLATE

Use a project tracking tool to host this in and stay on top of team progress and personal goals with a simple mental template. This is a simple tool for yourself personally to keep track of what is going on and who is doing what. And by when. As a lead you are not just keeping track of your own responsibilities, but those of your team. For project management on a bigger scale you would use something like a Gantt chart or other similar project tracking templates and software. This template is for a more general team overview.

Task	Owner	Status	Deadline	Notes
Finalize team report	Sarah	In Progress	June 15	Needs client feedback
Prepare team meeting agenda	You	Completed	June 12	Sent to team
Schedule team training	John	Not Started	June 20	Confirm trainer availability

How to use it:
- Weekly Review - identify priorities at the start of the week.
- Daily updates - track progress and adjust as needed.
- Team transparency - share relevant sections during check-ins.

THE ABCDE METHOD

When faced with a long list of tasks, it's easy to feel overwhelmed. The ABCDE Prioritization Method provides a straightforward approach to managing your responsibilities by assigning each task a level of importance:

- A. Must-Do Tasks - these are critical tasks with serious consequences if not completed. For example, preparing for a major presentation or addressing a critical team issue.
- B. Important but Not Critical - these tasks are significant but don't carry immediate consequences. An example might be developing a new team training program.
- C. Nice-to-Do Tasks - these activities are pleasant but have no real impact on your goals. Planning team-building events could fall under this category.
- D. Delegate - these tasks can be handled by someone else, freeing up your time for more important responsibilities.
- E. Eliminate - these are unnecessary tasks that can be removed from your to-do list entirely.

By categorizing your tasks using the ABCDE method, you gain clarity on where to focus your efforts and which tasks can be delegated or eliminated, making your workload more manageable and aligned with your priorities.

TIME-BLOCKING

Imagine having dedicated blocks of time solely for your most important tasks. The Time-Blocking Technique allows you to schedule specific periods in your calendar for focused work, strategic planning, or key projects. Here's how to implement it:

Start by blocking off hours in your calendar for deep work sessions. During these blocks, eliminate all distractions and concentrate on high-priority tasks. For example, reserve the first two hours of your day for strategic planning or complex problem-solving when your mind is freshest.

Next, allocate time for routine tasks and meetings separately. This ensures that administrative duties don't encroach on your time for critical work. By creating a structured schedule, you reduce the temptation to multitask and improve your overall focus and efficiency.

Time-blocking combines the principles of prioritization with disciplined execution, helping you stay on track and make significant progress on your most important goals.

THE MOSCOW METHOD

When managing projects, it's essential to prioritize tasks to ensure that critical elements are addressed first. The MoSCoW Method (devised by Dai Clegg) offers a clear framework by categorizing tasks into four groups:

- Must-haves are essential tasks that are crucial for achieving your goals.
- Should-haves are important tasks that add significant value but are not critical.
- Could-haves are nice additions that can be included if time permits.
- Won't-haves are tasks that are not necessary at this time but may be revisited later.

This method provides clarity in decision-making, especially when dealing with complex projects or competing demands. By clearly defining what needs to be prioritized, you ensure that your efforts are focused on the most impactful tasks, enhancing both efficiency and effectiveness.

THE 2-MINUTE RULE: HANDLE SMALL TASKS IMMEDIATELY

Sometimes, minor tasks can pile up and consume valuable mental space. The 2-Minute Rule (popularised by GoT master David Allen) offers a simple solution: if a task takes less than two minutes to complete, do it right away. Whether it's responding to a quick email, making a brief phone call, or handling a small administrative task, addressing it immediately prevents it from becoming a lingering burden.

For tasks that take longer than two minutes, decide whether to defer, delegate, or schedule them for later. This approach helps you keep your to-do list manageable and ensures that small tasks don't accumulate, allowing you to focus on more substantial responsibilities.

EAT THE FROG: TACKLE THE TOUGHEST TASK FIRST

Starting your day with the most challenging or important task can set a productive tone for the rest of the day. The Eat That Frog! technique (based on a quote by Mark Twain and popularized by Brian Tracy) encourages you to identify the task you're most likely to procrastinate on but has the highest impact, and commit to completing it first thing in the morning.

For example, if you dread preparing a comprehensive report, tackle it first thing after you start your day. By getting it done early, you build momentum and reduce mental resistance, making it easier to handle other tasks with greater ease and efficiency.

THE RACI MATRIX

Effective leadership requires clear roles and responsibilities within your team. (Likely originally used by the US Navy and popularised by the Project Management Institute in the 70s.) The RACI Matrix helps you achieve this by defining who is Responsible, Accountable, Consulted, and Informed for each task or project:

- Responsible: the person(s) who do the work.
- Accountable: the person ultimately answerable for the task's completion.
- Consulted: those who provide input or expertise.
- Informed: those who need to be kept updated on progress.

By clearly delineating roles, the RACI Matrix reduces confusion, streamlines collaboration, and ensures accountability, making your team more efficient and effective.

THE IVY LEE METHOD

The Ivy Lee Method (by a consultant named Ivy Lee from the 1910s) is a simple yet powerful technique for prioritizing your daily tasks. At the end of each day, list the six most important tasks you need to accomplish the next day. Rank them in order of priority and commit to completing the first task before moving on to the next. This focused approach prevents task-switching and enhances your ability to achieve key objectives.

For example, if your top task is to finalize a project proposal, dedicate your morning to completing it without distractions. Once it's done, move on to the next task with the same level of commitment and focus.

PARKINSON'S LAW

Parkinson's Law (from a satirical essay in The Economist by Cyril Northcote Parkinson) states that work expands to fill the time available for its completion. By setting shorter deadlines for tasks, you can improve your efficiency and prevent overcomplicating solutions. For instance, if a task typically takes three hours, challenge yourself to complete it in two. This approach forces you to focus and streamline your efforts, leading to more efficient use of your time.

Additionally, limit the duration of meetings and discussions to keep them concise and purposeful. By imposing time constraints, you enhance your ability to work swiftly and effectively, avoiding unnecessary delays and boosting overall productivity.

A NOTE ON TOOLS FOR PRODUCTIVITY

Productivity tools are constantly evolving, with new options emerging to address specific challenges leaders face. While the exact tools may change over time, the purpose behind them remains the same: to simplify workflows, enhance collaboration, and boost efficiency. Instead of focusing on finding the "perfect" tool, prioritize those that align with your current needs and fulfill a specific purpose.

For example, if your challenge is managing time effectively, look for calendar tools that allow you to organize your schedule seamlessly. If team collaboration is your focus, task management platforms or real-time document editing tools might be the answer. By keeping the purpose in mind—whether it's time tracking, focus enhancement, or team coordination—you can adapt to changes in technology while staying grounded in what truly supports your leadership goals.

Experiment with a few options, gather feedback from your team, and remain flexible as you integrate these tools into your daily routines. Over time, you'll develop a digital toolkit tailored to your leadership style, one that evolves with both your needs and advancements in technology.

PART 4:
TECH TOOLS FOR PRODUCTIVITY

Beyond current tools like Trello, Asana, and Notion, there is a vast array of productivity applications designed to cater to different aspects of leadership and team management. Exploring and integrating these tools can further streamline your workflow, enhance collaboration, and ensure you remain focused on your leadership priorities. Remember - these tools change over time and everyone has their favorite. What we have tried to do is to bring out examples of tools that fit a certain need, there are varieties available. A lot of these tools may have been chosen for you by your organisation already, in that case take this guide as a reminder of how these tools can be helpful for you instead of a hindrance. If you are in a very small team you may have more use from starting to use something like a CRM, in a big team that will have been taken care of for you already.

Managing emails in your inbox efficiently starts with setting up filters to automatically sort messages, keeping your inbox focused on what truly matters. Prioritize important emails by directing newsletters, promotions, and low-priority messages into separate folders. Instead of constantly monitoring your inbox, schedule specific times to check and respond to emails—this minimizes distractions and helps you stay focused on meaningful work.

Keyboard shortcuts are one of the simplest ways to speed up everyday tasks. Whether you're managing email, organizing tasks, or navigating between tools, learning just a few time-saving commands can make your workflow noticeably smoother. For example, pressing **C** to compose in Gmail or **Ctrl + Shift + M** to draft a new message in Outlook saves you clicks and time. In tools like Trello or Asana, shortcuts like **N** to add a new task or @ to assign it keep momentum going. Start with the shortcuts for the tools you use most, and let muscle memory do the rest.

Calendar Management for efficient scheduling is crucial for any leader. Tools like Google Calendar and Outlook Calendar offer robust features for organizing meetings, setting reminders, and sharing calendars with your team. These platforms allow you to block out dedicated times for deep work, meetings, and personal breaks, ensuring that your day is well-structured and balanced.

Note-taking and organization for keeping track of ideas, meeting notes, and important information is essential. Evernote and Microsoft OneNote provide versatile environments for capturing thoughts, organizing documents, and synchronizing notes across multiple devices. These tools enable you to maintain a centralized repository of information that is easily accessible and searchable.

Time tracking for understanding how you and your team spend time can lead to more effective time management. Toggl and Harvest offer intuitive interfaces for tracking time spent on various tasks and projects. These insights help identify areas where time can be better allocated, ultimately boosting productivity and efficiency.

Automation and integration for reducing repetitive tasks through automation can save significant time. Zapier and IFTTT (If This Then That) allow you to connect different apps and automate workflows without needing advanced technical skills. For example, you can set up automatic notifications for task completions or synchronize data between your project management and communication tools, minimizing manual updates and errors. AI assistants can also handle repetitive scheduling or even offer quick content ideas to make the workflows smoother. Bottom line is that the technology is constantly evolving and so should you.

File sharing for seamless collaboration is vital for team success. Google Drive, Dropbox, and Microsoft OneDrive facilitate easy sharing and real-time collaboration on documents, spreadsheets, and presentations. These platforms ensure that your team can work together efficiently, regardless of their physical location, and that all files are securely stored and accessible.

Real-time communication tools like Slack or Microsoft Teams help streamline collaboration by keeping discussions organized and easily accessible. Instead of scheduling unnecessary meetings, teams can quickly share updates, ask questions, and make decisions within dedicated channels. This not only saves time but also ensures that important conversations and files are readily available for reference, improving overall workflow efficiency. Just remember to mute channels and conversations that are not relevant.

Maintaining focus amidst numerous distractions is a common challenge. Tools like Freedom, Forest, and Focus@Will help you create distraction-free environments by blocking non-essential websites, encouraging productive breaks, and providing background music designed to enhance concentration. Incorporating these tools into your routine can significantly improve your ability to concentrate on high-priority tasks.

Meeting scheduling. Coordinating meeting times can be time-consuming. Calendly and Doodle simplify the scheduling process by allowing team members to select available time slots that work for everyone. These tools eliminate the back-and-forth emails typically involved in finding suitable meeting times, making the scheduling process more efficient and less stressful.

Customer Relationship Management (CRM) for managing relationships with clients and stakeholders is streamlined with CRM tools like Salesforce and HubSpot. These platforms help you track interactions, manage sales pipelines, and analyze customer data, enabling you to build stronger, more informed relationships and make data-driven decisions.

Mind mapping and brainstorming for visualizing ideas and strategies can enhance creativity and planning. MindMeister and

XMind offer intuitive interfaces for creating mind maps, allowing you to organize thoughts, explore connections, and develop comprehensive plans. These tools are particularly useful during brainstorming sessions and strategic planning meetings.

Advanced task management platforms like Monday.com and ClickUp provide extensive features for tracking projects, assigning tasks, and monitoring progress. These tools offer customizable workflows, automation options, and detailed reporting, ensuring that all aspects of your projects are managed efficiently and transparently.

Finding the right technology is about simplifying your workflow, not overcomplicating it. The specific tools you choose matter less than how well they support your needs. Start by identifying one small automation—whether it's an email filter, a recurring task reminder, or an auto-generated report—to build momentum toward continuous improvement. Stay curious, remain open to new solutions, and refine your digital toolkit to support both your leadership growth and your team's success. And don't forget to bookmark the ones you use most!

PART 5:
LEVERAGING AI RESPONSIBLY

This is written in 2025 so by the time you read it: most likely some of it will be out of date. Artificial intelligence has moved from novelty to everyday assistant in about the time it takes to brew a coffee. For a first-time lead it unlocks small but meaningful advantages that compound across a busy week. This part shows how to tap those gains without crossing the lines of privacy, ethics, or common sense. It also explains how AI helped create this workbook: large-language-model drafts were used for early ideation, then every chapter was rewritten, fact checked, and edited by real humans to keep the voice and the data trustworthy. We asked AI for feedback and clarity, for how sectioning makes sense and to help find all the relevant references to the tools we like using. We are both non-native english speakers so having AI to reflect back and correct issues in our actual language use was very helpful

Quick wins that AI can help with.

- Draft meeting agendas in seconds by feeding yesterday's chat transcript to an LLM.
- Summarise one-on-one notes into action items and emoji-level mood signals.
- Run a first-pass data analysis—trend lines, outliers, questions for deeper dives—before you call in the analyst.
- Turn a rough idea into a clear email or stakeholder brief without staring at a blank page.

Guardrails you need to use

- Privacy: strip personal data before sharing files with external tools.
- Hallucinations: verify every fact that matters; treat AI output as a confident intern, not gospel.
- Bias: ask for multiple perspectives and run inclusive language checks.
- Transparency: tell your team when AI touched the work so nobody feels deceived.

MINI EXERCISES

1. Copy three sets of meeting notes into your favourite LLM and request a five-sentence summary plus bullet action items. compare with your own summary. Where did the machine add value? Where did it miss nuance?

2. Paste a customer email thread into the tool and ask it to generate two reply options: one concise, one empathetic. Discuss with a colleague which tone fits the relationship.

3. Give the model this prompt: "list five low-risk tasks a new lead could automate this quarter." Test one suggestion and report back in your next one-on-one.

Great leaders rarely have every answer; they define clear goals that draw the best solutions from the team. Treat AI the same way. Frame your requests around desired outcomes rather than prescribing every detail. Describe the destination, not the route, for example, "Find the three customer segments most likely to upgrade" instead of asking, "Which audience should we target?". State constraints such as budget, tone, deadlines, and compliance rules up front. Iterate with the model as you would with a junior teammate: critique the draft, refine it, and keep adding context until the output clicks. Maintain accountability by logging prompts and decisions so the rest of the group can learn and the model stays within policy.

Think of AI as an additional team member: fast and tireless yet still needing direction. Your role is to orchestrate effective collaboration. Pair a human reviewer with every critical AI deliverable, rotate ownership of prompting tasks to build skill across the team, and celebrate successes from both sides, the analyst who spotted a data glitch and the bot that flagged it first.

Ask yourself:

- Which part of your day drains energy that AI could refill?
- Where does only a human voice earn trust?
- How will you make sure transparency and quality stay high as automation grows?

CHAPTER 3:
MASTERING ONE-ON-ONE MEETINGS

In this chapter, you'll learn how to make one-on-one meetings (often called 1:1s) one of the most effective tools in your leadership toolkit. We'll walk through the purpose behind them, how to prepare and structure them, and how to use them to build trust, offer support, and drive growth.

How often you should have a 1:1 with your team member depends on what kind of work you do, if there is a current project, is the employee very new or experienced, what other responsibilities the team has and so on. It can also change in time depending on all these variables. What I can say is that it is not enough to do it once a year. Would you rather not find out someone is heading in the wrong direction faster than once per year? Would you rather not help course correct more often?

PART 1:
WHY 1:1s MATTER

Great leadership isn't built in group meetings or status updates—it's built in the quiet, consistent rhythm of one-on-one conversations. 1:1s are where you earn trust, hear the things that don't come up in public, and coach your team toward long-term growth.

These meetings might seem simple on the surface, but when used well, they become one of the most impactful leadership habits you can develop. If you've never had a great 1:1 modeled for you, that's okay—this chapter will help you build that skill from the ground up.

One-on-one meetings matter because they create a safe space for honest conversations, show your team you care about their input and growth, allow early identification and resolution of challenges, ensure alignment on priorities and direction, and provide a platform for ongoing coaching and career development.

PART 2:
WHAT MAKES A GREAT 1:1

Before jumping into templates or questions, it's essential to understand the foundation of impactful 1:1s. There are several important elements that turn these conversations from routine check-ins into powerful tools for trust-building and development.

THE CORE PRINCIPLES

- Consistency. Set a recurring schedule—weekly or biweekly depending on the team's needs. A newer team or high-complexity project may call for more frequent check-ins. No matter what you decide, treat this time as sacred. Only reschedule if absolutely necessary. If the team is in a particularly busy season, reduce frequency to monthly or bimonthly, but return to normal cadence once the workload allows. This signals to your team that their growth and support remain a priority, even under pressure.
- Preparation. Work from both parties ensures that time is used well. Unplanned meetings often drift off-course or feel rushed. Use a shared agenda or collaborative document where both you and the team member can add discussion points ahead of time. This sets expectations and encourages shared ownership of the meeting.
- Presence. Being physically in the room or on a call isn't enough. To make a 1:1 meaningful, you need to be mentally and emotionally present too. That means eliminating distractions (like phones and notifications), maintaining eye contact, and listening with intention. Your focus shows your team that they matter.

- Set a cadence that makes sense for the context. Not every team needs the same rhythm. A brand-new hire might benefit from weekly 1:1s, while a long-tenured employee might thrive with biweekly sessions. Pay attention to the evolving needs of your team, and communicate any changes transparently.
- Create and maintain an agenda. Encourage team members to contribute to it regularly. A shared document, perhaps one of the tools mentioned in Chapter 2, helps make sure important topics aren't missed. Here's what a typical agenda could include:
   - o Updates on current projects and responsibilities
   - o Challenges or obstacles they're facing
   - o Feedback: both giving and receiving
   - o Career development conversations
   - o A quick check-in on overall well-being or work-life balance
- While project updates are important, they should never take over the full conversation. Be sure there's space for deeper topics, like growth and feedback.
- Review your notes from past meetings. Before heading into your next 1:1, skim through previous action items, comments, or follow-ups. This helps you hold continuity and demonstrate that you're actively tracking what matters to your team member. It also shows you value their time and input.

TAKING NOTES

During the meeting, make it a habit to jot down key points, commitments, and any feedback shared. This isn't just for your benefit, it's also a signal that you're listening and treating the conversation seriously. After the meeting:

- Spend a few minutes cleaning up your notes.
- Organize them into themes or action steps.
- Share any agreed-upon action items.

This kind of thoughtful follow-up builds mutual accountability. It also reduces miscommunication and can become especially useful if you ever need to revisit conversations down the line.

PART 3:
HOW TO RUN THEM

Now that we've covered why 1:1s matter and how to prepare, let's get into how to run them effectively. While flexibility is important, having a clear structure ensures that each meeting delivers value for both you and your team member.

SUGGESTED STRUCTURE

1. Personal Check-In (5–10 minutes)

Start with something open and genuine—"How are you feeling this week?" or "What's been on your mind lately?" This moment is more than small talk—it builds trust. Keep the door open for both personal and professional insights. Some people will want to share a lot; others less. Follow their lead, but always make space for it.

2. Project Updates (10–15 minutes)

Cover current responsibilities, timelines, and priorities. Acknowledge wins and progress. This section isn't about micromanaging—it's about alignment. Recognize their achievements so they know their work is seen and valued.

3. Challenges and Roadblocks (10–15 minutes)

Ask what's been hard lately. You might say, "What's been most challenging in your work?" or "Is there anything you're stuck on that I can help with?" It's your job to help remove barriers. Offer support, ideas, or resources—but listen fully first. Sometimes just hearing them out already lightens the burden.

---

4. Development and Growth (10–15 minutes)

This is where the real magic happens. Ask about long-term goals, interests, or areas they'd like to grow in. Don't assume you know what motivates them—ask. You might ask, "What's something new you'd like to try?" or "Is there a skill you want to develop this quarter?" Link feedback or stretch assignments to these aspirations.

5. Wrap-Up (5 minutes)

Recap what you discussed, confirm next steps, and make sure action items are clear. It can be helpful to say, "So just to wrap up, here's what we agreed on..." After the meeting, send a short written summary—especially when there are key commitments involved. This avoids misunderstandings and reinforces accountability.

TIPS FOR STRONG EXECUTION

- Be fully present: Don't split attention. Close extra tabs, silence your phone, and avoid multitasking. If you need to take notes, let them know why so it's not mistaken for disengagement. If possible take notes by hand, computers and phones create a barrier between you.

- Ask open-ended questions: These invite real conversation. Avoid yes/no formats. Try, "What's something you're proud of this week?" or "What would make your work easier right now?" (More on that in Chapter 6 about coaching)

- Don't fake interest: People can spot insincerity. If you're not curious, take a breath and reset. Come in with a coaching mindset.

- Be flexible: Sometimes a topic will take up more time than planned. That's okay. Stay human and responsive.

- Consider the format: Not everyone thrives in a sit-down setting. Some people open up better while walking or over a coffee. Try different formats to see what suits each person best. A sit-down is a less common format, but it's very useful when a new team is getting up to speed and at the start of new projects.

In day-to-day work, a more typical cadence is a quick 15-minute stand-up on Monday and another on Friday. On Monday, each team member shares what they plan to accomplish that week; on Friday, they report what they actually achieved and explain any gaps. This rhythm is especially helpful for you as the team lead because it gives you a clear picture of how the team is progressing—and if it isn't, why. What you do with that information next is a key step in your leadership skill set, which we cover throughout this book.

A common pitfall is doing all the talking. This is a frequent trap—especially when you're busy or enthusiastic. But if you fill every silence or steer every topic, your team member misses the chance to share what matters most to them. Try asking, then pausing. Use silence as a tool. Jot down your thoughts rather than interrupting. Reflect their words back to ensure understanding. This signals you care, and it builds a space where people feel safe, heard, and empowered to contribute. Learn to simply sit in silence and listen while giving time for the other person to get clarity in their head. Silence does not have to uncomfortable, it is time for your conversation partner to set things straight in their head.

PART 4:
FEEDBACK IN 1:1s

At the heart of every impactful 1:1 is a strong feedback culture. Feedback should not be treated as something formal or saved for yearly reviews. It is a continuous dialogue that happens during your everyday interactions—and 1:1s are one of the best times to cultivate it.

In its simplest form, feedback is information—positive, constructive, or corrective—that helps someone understand how they are doing and where they can improve. When done well, feedback supports learning, strengthens trust, and keeps performance aligned with expectations and goals.

1:1s provide the perfect rhythm for timely, relevant feedback. You don't have to wait for something big to happen—small, thoughtful feedback in the moment (or in your next scheduled 1:1) builds confidence, clarity, and momentum.

HOW TO GIVE FEEDBACK THAT LANDS

- Be specific and timely. Vague praise or criticism isn't useful. "Good job" doesn't tell them what worked. Instead, say: "I appreciated the way you stayed calm and organized during the client call. Your summary helped us land the next step."
- Balance appreciation with opportunities for growth. Always lead with something you genuinely appreciate. Then, gently offer an area for improvement. This balance keeps people open to growth while feeling supported. For example: "Your report was very thorough—next time, consider tightening up the structure to make it easier to follow."
- Frame it as a conversation. You're not giving a performance review—you're having a dialogue. Ask questions like, "How do you think that went?" or "What do you feel worked best?" This makes feedback feel like a shared exploration, not a judgment.
- Link it to goals. If someone has expressed a desire to grow in a certain area, tailor your feedback to that. For example: "Since you mentioned wanting to lead more meetings, I thought the way you handled the agenda today was a great step in that direction."

RECEIVING FEEDBACK AS A LEAD

This might feel uncomfortable at first—but asking for feedback from your team is essential. It models the behavior you want from them, and it helps you improve. Many new leaders worry about looking vulnerable, but the opposite is true: being open earns respect.

Here's how to invite it:

- Ask directly. Try questions like, "What's something I could be doing better?" or "Is there anything I can do to make our 1:1s more helpful for you?"
- Listen with curiosity, not defensiveness. Feedback may not always feel nice, but it's always useful. If something stings, take a breath and thank them for their honesty. You can always reflect and follow up later.
- Act on what you hear. Nothing erodes trust faster than asking for feedback and ignoring it. Even small changes show you're listening. Circle back to let them know what you've tried, or why you made a decision differently.

CREATING A CULTURE OF TWO-WAY FEEDBACK

When feedback is a regular, safe part of your 1:1s, your team learns that speaking up is not risky: it's welcome. And the more feedback flows in both directions, the more you'll understand what your team needs to thrive.

This also helps you spot patterns early, before problems grow or misunderstandings harden. When feedback becomes normal, it's no longer about "fixing issues," it's about growing together.

It's not about perfection. It's about progress, honesty, and shared accountability.

If someone gives you feedback that triggers doubt or insecurity, take it to your own lead. Use your support system too, you're learning, and that's okay.

A strong feedback culture doesn't happen overnight, but every 1:1 is an opportunity to move closer to it. And over time, it becomes a natural part of how your team communicates, improves, and grows together.

PART 5:
EXERCISE AND REFLECTION

BUILD YOUR PERSONAL 1:1 FRAMEWORK

Creating your own repeatable structure is the best way to put this chapter into practice. A solid framework not only keeps your meetings focused and valuable, but also gives your team a consistent experience they can trust.

Start by setting up a shared document or template with these core sections. Use it collaboratively—both you and your team member can add thoughts ahead of time.

- **Check-in.** A quick look into personal well-being, energy, or highlights from the week. Opens the space with empathy.
- **Updates.** A review of progress on key projects or deliverables. Focus on alignment, not micromanagement.
- **Challenges.** Any blockers or roadblocks they're facing. This is your time to listen and offer support.
- **Feedback.** Space for ongoing performance feedback— both giving and receiving. Keep it timely and constructive.
- **Development.** Discuss career goals, new skills, and stretch opportunities. Support their long-term growth.
- **Action Items.** Wrap up by clearly noting next steps, responsibilities, and deadlines. Follow-through builds trust.

1:1s are a long-term leadership habit. Don't just focus on one meeting: look for patterns, relationships, and progress.

Every month or two, take 15–30 minutes and ask yourself:
- Are these 1:1s helping my team feel supported and seen?
- Am I learning what motivates and challenges each person?
- Have I been giving and receiving feedback consistently?
- What could I adjust—timing, structure, tone—to make these more impactful?

This kind of self-review helps keep your 1:1s alive and relevant—not just another calendar event. Making reflection a habit for everything you do in life helps you take a step back and align yourself on the right path. How to take that time and keep it for what you want and not what others dictate - that is the topic of the next chapter.

CHAPTER 4:
"IT COULD HAVE BEEN AN EMAIL"

As a new leader, you might notice your calendar filling up at an alarming speed. Meetings often feel like an unavoidable part of leadership—useful for connecting with your team, making decisions, and keeping projects on track. But they can also become overwhelming. Jumping from one meeting to another leaves little time for the tasks that demand deeper focus, creativity, or strategic thinking.

Remember: not every issue needs a meeting. And when a meeting is necessary, it doesn't always require every team member. Each 10 person meeting that lasts an hour is actually 10 hours of work that was not done.

In this chapter, you will learn how to:

- Recognize and prevent unnecessary meetings that waste valuable time and energy.
- Evaluate your own meeting habits and discern whether a meeting is genuinely needed—or if an email or shared document could be more efficient.
- Implement practical strategies to protect your calendar, reduce meeting overload, and make room for high-priority work.
- Explore alternative approaches, such as co-working sessions, shorter meeting formats, and asynchronous communication.
- Engage your team in improving meeting culture, including how to gather useful feedback on scheduling and meeting effectiveness.

Before we dive in, let's begin with a short, reflective exercise to prime your thinking about your own meeting practices.

PART 1:
CHANGING YOUR MIND ABOUT MEETINGS

THE HIDDEN COST OF MEETINGS

Meetings are like salt: a bit enhances the flavor, but too much ruins the meal. Yes, they're crucial for collaboration and ensuring everyone is on the same page, but not every topic requires gathering the whole team. Each unnecessary meeting saps energy, disrupts productivity, and can leave you wondering where the day went.

As a leader, being intentional about scheduling (and even attending) meetings is critical. Not every issue needs a meeting, and not every meeting needs the entire team in the room. Think about it: an hour-long meeting with ten people equals ten hours of productivity lost. That adds up quickly, leading to missed deadlines and stalled projects.

Before scheduling a meeting, ask yourself: "Is this meeting necessary, or could we handle this through email, a quick message, or a shared document?" By treating meeting time as valuable currency, you help create a culture that respects everyone's workload and improves overall efficiency.

ARE YOU SEEKING ACCOUNTABILITY OR AVOIDING WORK?

There's one honest question to consider: Are you scheduling or joining so many meetings because it's the only time you feel accountable and productive? Sometimes, we use meetings to avoid the discomfort of doing deep, solo work. You're not alone if you find yourself scrolling your phone or procrastinating when working independently.

When we wrote this book, we noticed we accomplished far more when we were in the same room together—actually writing—rather than discussing what needed to be done. That accountability of working side by side often replaced the need for a formal "meeting." If you recognize yourself in this scenario, try scheduling co-working sessions instead. Gather in the same space (or virtual call) and agree: "We're here to work on individual tasks, not hold a meeting." It satisfies the need for accountability without turning into a distraction-heavy discussion.

I've personally found co-working especially helpful. For instance, I'll work on dreaded accounting tasks while a friend tackles their overflowing inbox. Just having someone else being productive nearby helps me focus. You can do the same at home: if I need to clean and my friend needs to finish a school assignment, we occupy the same room, each handling our tasks. It's surprisingly motivating to have that mutual "let's get this done" energy, without calling it an official meeting.

PART 2:
THE "DO YOU REALLY NEED THAT MEETING?" FRAMEWORK

To help you determine if you truly need a meeting— or if email, a shared document, or co-working might do—walk through these five steps. They'll save you time and prevent your team from experiencing meeting overload.

STEP-BY-STEP GUIDE

1: Reflect on the Issue Independently

Before hitting "send" on that calendar invite, ask yourself if you've really brainstormed on your own. Sometimes, personal reflection or quick research can answer your questions without involving others.

2: Do You Actually Need Outside Input?

If you're seeking someone else's buy-in or expertise, great—but be sure that's essential. Remember, soliciting open-ended "thoughts" can invite a flood of irrelevant commentary. A more effective approach: Ask for objections or specific feedback if you do need input. If you don't need others' perspectives, stick to solo work.

3: Could This Be Handled Asynchronously?

If back-and-forth discussion isn't urgent or complex, skip the live gathering. An email, a shared document, or a chat thread might suffice—and people can contribute when they have time. This is particularly helpful if your team is distributed across time zones or busy with diverse tasks.

4: Could a Quick Phone Call or Message Work Instead?

If the topic demands real-time interaction but doesn't require everyone to be present, consider a brief call or message. Video conferences often eat up just as much time as in-person meetings, so a phone call is sometimes faster.

5: Finally, Schedule the Real Meeting

If you've gone through all the above and still see a clear need for a real-time, same-place discussion, go ahead and book it. From experience, about 80% of the meetings you think you need can be worked through more effectively with one of the first four steps.

Pick a meeting you're about to schedule—or one you suspect might be superfluous. Ask yourself the five questions above. If it fails any of these tests, shift it to an email, a quick call, or a co-working session.

PART 3:
PRACTICAL STRATEGIES, EXERCISES & NEXT STEPS

GUARD YOUR CALENDAR

Managing your meetings effectively starts with protecting your essential time. Block out spots on your calendar for lunch, short breaks, and focus work. Leave 15-minute buffers between back-to-back calls so you can mentally switch gears, jot down notes, or handle urgent tasks that pop up. These small adjustments help keep fatigue at bay and ensure you're consistently bringing your best to every conversation. Remember the prioritisation exercises from Chapter 2? This is what you need to make time for in your calendar, the impactful things that move you forward. You do not have to go to every meeting simply because you were invited, will that meeting help with your results and impact or is it a nice way to spend time and feel important?

It's also wise to audit your calendar regularly. At the start of each week, review every upcoming meeting with a critical eye.

- Do you personally need to be present?
- Could a team member substitute for you?
- Is a recurring meeting still serving its original purpose, or can you cancel or combine it?

By routinely examining your schedule, you free up precious time for high-priority tasks that actually need your attention.

As a leader, you set the tone for your team's meeting culture. When you do schedule a meeting, always share a clear agenda. That way, participants know how to prepare and stay focused on the goal. Also question the default length: not every discussion requires a full hour. Try shorter 15- or 30-minute sessions to cut down on filler and keep energy high. Remember Parkinson's Law? Work will fill the amount of time set aside for it. If you had an hour booked and got all the important things done in 30 minutes, I guarantee the other 3o minutes will get filled with useless nonsense. Book shorter meetings to motivate people to be on point and execute.

Exploring alternatives to conventional meetings can save you and your team plenty of hours. Detailed written updates via email or shared docs often work just as well for routine check-ins. Tools like Trello, Asana, and Slack let teams collaborate and contribute asynchronously, freeing the calendar of repetitive status meetings. If you only need to chat with one person, a quick one-on-one call is often far more efficient than gathering a crowd.

Weekly Standups and Sitdowns

- **Standups.** Each team member quickly shares what they're working on, flags any blockers, and requests help if needed. These keep momentum going and highlight small issues before they escalate.
- **Sitdowns.** At the week's end, gather briefly to reflect on accomplishments, discuss any lingering hurdles, and align on next week's goals.

Both formats are quick but informative, ensuring everyone feels in sync without an endless parade of formal meetings. Some teams with a lot of ambiguity have daily standups to keep on point and make quick changes in navigating. It helps with alignment. You will know if your team is one of those if it had pre-existing daily standups. If you do some sort of project or event work, you may need a weekly meeting in the beginning stages of a project, but need to move it daily as the big day approaches. Rule of thumb is that if you meet once a week for a Monday status meeting and it is full of complaints about how something important was not done on

Wednesday last week - you need to have a daily check-in.

EXERCISES TO OPTIMIZE YOUR TIME

1. Reflect on Last Week's Meetings
   - Were they necessary?
   - Could they have been condensed or replaced by an email or Slack thread?
   - Identify at least one you can modify or cut outright going forward.

2. Block Your Calendar for Next Week.
   - Refer to your priorities from 80/20 and make time for the 20% of things with the most impact.
   - Schedule protected times for high-focus tasks, lunches, and short breaks.
   - Label these blocks clearly so others know you're unavailable.
   - If someone tries to schedule over them, politely explain why you must protect that time.

3. Gather Team Feedback

   Encourage your team to share ideas for making meetings more effective:
   - "Which part of our meetings feels most valuable?"
   - "What changes could make them more engaging or efficient?"
   - "Could any meeting topics be handled asynchronously?"

4. Even small improvements (like a tighter agenda or fewer attendees) can dramatically boost productivity and engagement.

MEETINGS ARE TOOLS, NOT TIME TRAPS

Ultimately, your time is extremely valuable. How you allocate it not only affects your own productivity, but also sets the pace for your entire team. Meetings should serve a clear purpose—facilitating progress, aligning the group, or making decisions. By managing your calendar and being selective about meetings, you free up space for strategic thinking, meaningful work, and needed breaks.

A helpful resource: Elizabeth Grace Saunders wrote a 2015 Harvard Business Review article with a flowchart on when to accept or decline a meeting. If you receive an invite with no agenda or outcome, you might share that link and ask the organizer: "Where exactly are we in this flowchart, and why do I need to attend?" Sometimes, the meeting gets canceled. Other times, the organizer realizes they need a real agenda—and the resulting discussion becomes far more productive.

Above all, approach meetings as tools to achieve specific goals, not as default obligations that chew up your schedule. By being intentional, embracing alternatives, and refining your process, you'll protect your time, empower your team, and lead more effectively. Taking control of your calendar is a powerful step toward taking control of your leadership journey.

Now, return to your "possibly unnecessary" meeting list from the reflection at the beginning for this chapter.

- Can you eliminate, shorten, or convert any of those?
- Which alternative—an email thread, shared doc, quick call, or co-working session—might serve you better?

By making even a few small changes, you'll see the difference in your team's morale and your own clarity of mind. Enjoy the extra time and energy to focus on truly important work!

CHAPTER 5:
LEARNING TO SAY NO

Learning to say no can feel intimidating, especially if you've always been recognized for being available and saying yes. Early in my career, I believed that being a top performer meant tackling every request that came my way. Eventually, I realized that by always saying yes, I was pushing myself toward burnout. Through that experience, I learned that carefully choosing when to refuse frees up time for what really matters, helps you stay energized, and allows others to develop their own strengths.

Saying no is vital because it protects your focus and helps prevent burnout. Each time you say yes, you're indirectly saying no to something else, often a task that is more important to your main goals. As a leader, part of your role is to direct time and energy toward projects that have the greatest long-term impact. When you're stretched too thin, you risk your own well-being and can slow your team's progress.

Setting aside downtime is not selfish: it's smart. It also serves as a positive example that personal balance is important. Saying no can give others room to learn and grow. By turning down requests that don't require your direct involvement, you open the door for someone else to sharpen their skills and gain confidence.

Being selective in what you commit to also builds credibility. Leaders who overcommit can appear unfocused, while those who decline requests for the right reasons show that they have clear priorities. It helps to briefly explain why you're declining, such as focusing on a more urgent project or pointing out that someone else might be better suited for the task. Over time, people will see you as someone who is decisive and intentional with your time.

Sometimes, requests arrive at the wrong moment, are outside your expertise, or clash with higher priorities. In these cases, a polite but firm refusal can protect your schedule and maintain good relationships. You might suggest other possibilities, like delegating to a colleague or asking clarifying questions. If you feel the timeline is too tight or the meeting has no clear purpose, speak up to guard your limited capacity.

POSSIBLE SCENARIOS AND HOW TO RESPOND

When you're overloaded with work

- Example phrase: "I appreciate the trust, but my schedule is booked. Could someone else handle this, or could we revisit it when I have more bandwidth?"
- Reflection question: Where do I most frequently get pulled away from my main priorities?

When a meeting lacks a clear agenda

- Example phrase: "Thanks for including me. May I see an agenda first? I'm focusing on priority tasks and want to ensure my presence is necessary."
- Reflection question: How often do I attend meetings that don't serve my top goals?

When a request is outside your expertise

- Example phrase: "That's a bit outside my main skill set. I recommend connecting with someone who has the right background for this."
- Reflection question: Who on my team can handle this better, and how can delegating help them grow?

When you need downtime (social or otherwise)

- Example phrase: "I'd love to join, but I really need some personal time to recharge. Let's catch up another time."
- Reflection question: Am I consistently carving out time to recharge so I can lead effectively?

When a client pushes for a rushed deadline

- Example phrase: "I understand the urgency, but this deadline might affect quality. Could we extend the timeline or adjust the scope?"
- Reflection question: Am I communicating enough about realistic timelines and quality expectations?

When a small favor distracts from core work

- Example phrase: "I'd love to help, but I need to stay focused on a top-priority project. Could someone else step in?"
- Reflection question: What tasks could I delegate to free up time for the most valuable work?

When a volunteer role doesn't align with your goals

- Example phrase: "Thanks for asking, but my focus is in a different area right now. I'm open to a one-time assist if needed, though."
- Reflection question: Which volunteer or side projects bring real value, and which ones are simply draining my time?

When someone relies on you too often

- Example phrase: "I know this matters to you, but I believe you can handle it. I need to focus on my tasks. If you get stuck, let's schedule a brief check-in."
- Reflection question: In what ways can encouraging others to find their own solutions improve their growth and my bandwidth?

Set aside regular time to match your commitments with your main goals. Notice where you feel most overwhelmed, and consider how saying no more strategically could help. It can also be useful to plan your "no" responses in advance so you can deliver them clearly and politely. Over time, you'll build a reputation for protecting your energy, respecting other people's boundaries, and focusing on what truly matters.

EXERCISE: STRENGTHENING YOUR ABILITY TO SAY NO

1. Reflect on Recent Overcommitments
   - Recall three situations where you agreed to something that led to overload.
   - For each situation, write down how you could have declined.
   - Think about how saying no in those moments might have improved the outcome, for you and others.

2. Conduct a Priority Audit (Chapter 2 exercises on priorities)
   - Make a quick list of your current tasks and responsibilities.
   - oIdentify at least one item that doesn't align well with your top objectives.
   - Decide whether you can delegate it or decline it entirely this week.

3. Practice Saying No
   - Find a mentor or friend and do a brief role-play where you turn down a request.
   - Focus on being calm, clear, and respectful as you decline.
   - Discuss afterward which parts felt natural and which parts were more challenging.

4. Check Your Alignment Regularly
   - Ask yourself often, "Am I saying yes to the right things?"
   - Remember that each time you say no to a distraction, you create room to say yes to what truly matters.

CHAPTER 6:
COACHING - YOUR ULTIMATE LEADERSHIP TOOL

In this chapter we explore coaching as one of the most powerful methods to help you grow as a new leader and you'll discover:

- Why coaching matters and how it transforms team dynamics
- Essential coaching tools (like SMART goals and the GROW model) and how to apply them
- Advanced techniques (such as 360-degree feedback and values assessments) to deepen team engagement
- Core coaching behaviors that make every conversation more impactful
- Strategies for asking powerful questions so you can guide, rather than direct, your team

By the end of this chapter, you'll understand how to integrate coaching practices into your day-to-day leadership, creating a growth-focused environment for both you and your team.

PART 1:
WHY COACHING MATTERS

The first time I saw coaching in action, I was quite skeptical. I've always been cautious about trendy ideas that claim to change everything overnight. But what I didn't realize then was that coaching wasn't some fleeting trend; it's a tool that has been refined over decades, evolving into a powerful method for unlocking human potential. Little did I know, it would completely reshape how I lead and how I view growth and connection.

Once I started using coaching in my leadership, my perspective changed. Rather than handing my team the answers, I invited them to discover their own solutions. This shift led to gains in confidence, creativity, and ownership. It wasn't just about completing tasks, it was about helping people flourish in ways I hadn't fully imagined before.

I became so inspired that I even considered pursuing a full-time coaching path and looked into an ICF certification. Life took me in a different direction, but the experience transformed my leadership and my worldview. Coaching not only improved how I lead - it reshaped my entire approach to growth and relationships, leaving a profound and lasting impact.

PART 2:
ESSENTIAL COACHING TOOLS

Now that you've seen why coaching matters, let's explore some essential coaching tools that can bring your leadership to life. Each tool offers a structured way to guide conversations, solve problems, and support your team's personal and professional growth. In this section, you'll learn how to set SMART goals, conduct GROW conversations, map out the Wheel of Life, perform a SWOT Analysis, and use Mind Mapping to unlock creativity.

SMART GOALS

Help your team set Specific, Measurable, Achievable, Relevant, and Time-bound goals. This framework, originally introduced by George T. Doran, makes objectives clear and actionable, paving the way for real progress.

Start by pinpointing exactly what you want to accomplish (that's the specific part). Then decide how to measure success (measurable), and make sure your aim is realistic yet challenging (achievable). Check that it matters to your overall direction (relevant), and finally, give it a deadline (time-bound). This framework keeps you focused and makes it easier to track real progress.

Try it out now, fill this in for a goal you and your team have right now.

Specific	Consider exactly what you want to achieve and who will be involved. Clearly outline the main purpose, identify where and when it should happen, and reflect on why it matters.
Measurable	Figure out how you'll gauge success. Decide which metrics or milestones will show you're moving toward your goal. If you're tackling a longer project, plan key steps to stay on course.
Achievable	Set goals that inspire you but still fit within your current abilities or resources. If you're missing a skill or tool, think about what it takes to acquire it.
Relevant	Make sure your goal supports broader objectives, whether it's a personal ambition or a company target. Check if the timing is right and that you're the appropriate person to see it through.
Time-based	Pick a realistic deadline to keep yourself and others motivated. Ask what can be completed within that timeframe and how you'll adjust if things change.

Specific	
Measurable	
Achievable	
Relevant	
Time-based	

GROW COACHING MODEL

GOALS

Clearly define what
you aim to achieve.

REALITY

Assess your current
situation objectively.

OPTIONS

Explore various strategies
or actions available

WAY FORWARD

Commit to actionable steps
and create a clear plan
for moving ahead.

GROW MODEL

Use the grow model to guide conversations clearly and effectively. It has four simple steps: goals, reality, options, and way forward. This method helps team members understand exactly what they want, recognize where they currently stand, identify different ways to achieve their objectives, and then decide on practical actions to move forward. It's a straightforward approach to making conversations productive and focused.

GOALS

_____

_____

_____

REALITY

_____

_____

_____

OPTIONS

_____

_____

_____

WAY FORWARD

_____

_____

_____

WHEEL OF LIFE

A self-assessment tool that lets your people evaluate key areas of their life—like career, relationships, and health—by visually mapping satisfaction levels. It's great for identifying where they feel fulfilled or where they might want more focus. Here is a filled in example showing you the process. The idea is to identify where you are most imbalanced and see what you can do about it. Sometimes you are pouring all your energy and power into a part of life that is already going well, and you can't understand why your life in general is not getting better. This is also ag great tool to understand why you do not have any energy to build - generally because you are trying to put all your power somewhere it is not needed instead of what most needs your attention and is dragging you down.

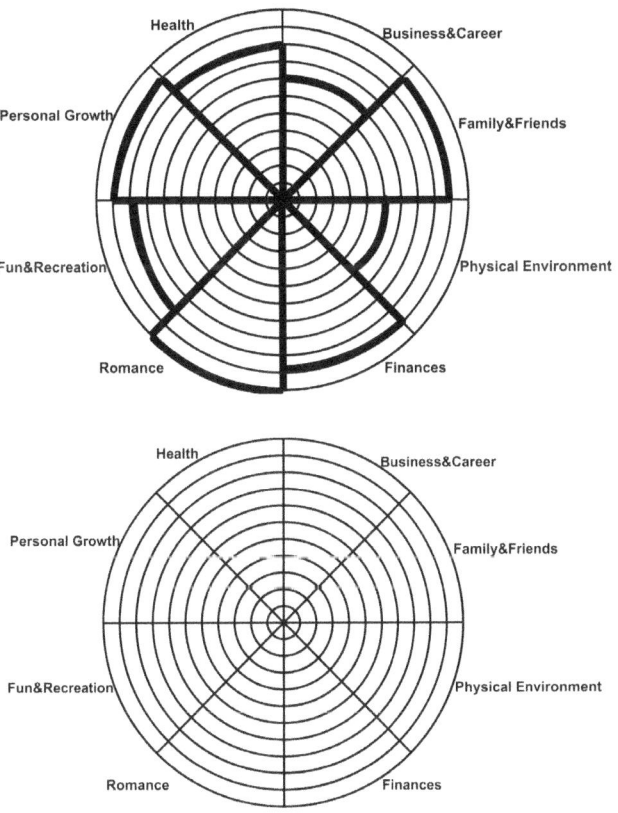

Use a swot analysis to help your team clearly see what they're good at (strengths), where they might struggle (weaknesses), what opportunities are out there to grow, and any possible risks or challenges (threats).

It's a simple tool for understanding what's happening inside your team, as well as what's going on around you. Doing this helps everyone make better decisions and plan effectively for the future.

STRENGTHS	WEAKNESSES

Internal advantages your team has.	Internal areas needing improvement.
OPPORTUNITIES	THREATS

External chances to grow or advance.	External challenges or risks.

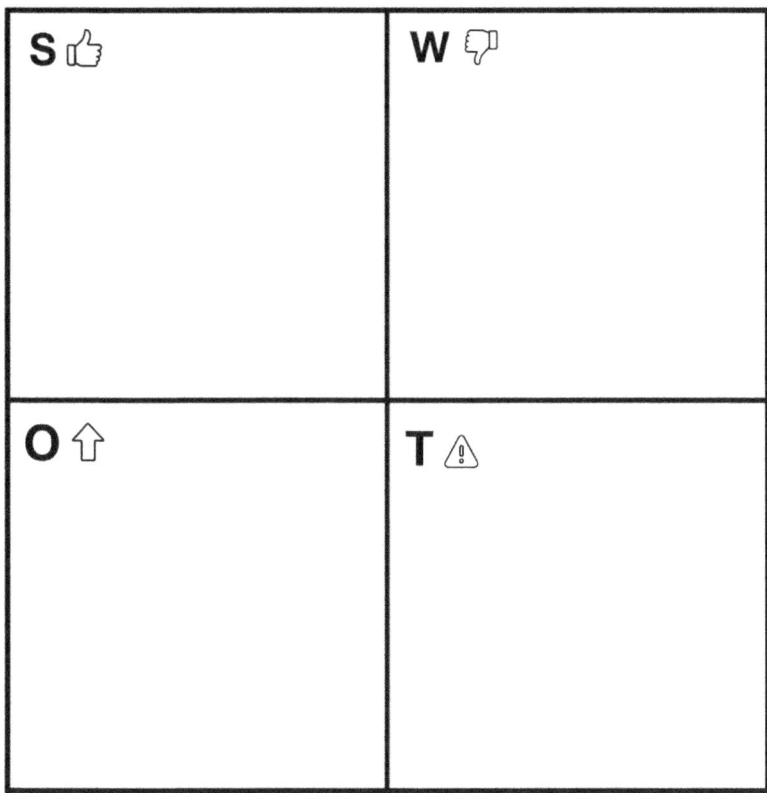

MIND MAPPING

A creative way to brainstorm and visually organize ideas. It's especially helpful for breaking down complex issues into clear steps or seeing connections between concepts. Place your main idea in the center of a blank page, then branch out with subtopics or related concepts around it. Draw lines to show how these elements connect, letting you spot hidden relationships as you visualize your thinking process.

Try one now. Take a topic you have been struggling with making progress and write that in the center. Then start filling in connected ideas.

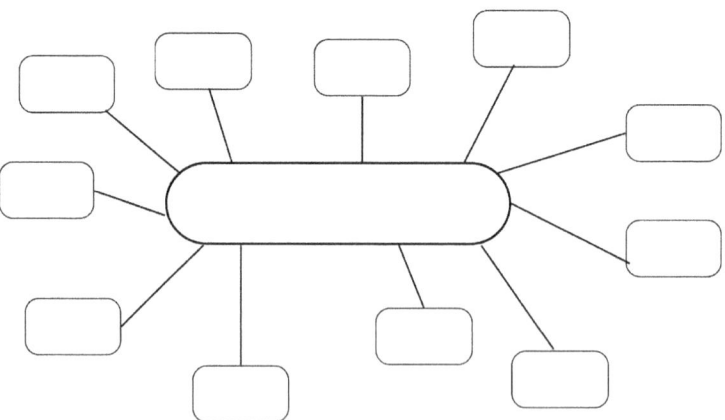

PART 3:
ADVANCED COACHING TOOLS

You've now explored the essential coaching tools—like SMART goals, the GROW model, and SWOT analyses—that form a strong foundation for your leadership. Let's build on that foundation by diving into advanced coaching tools that offer deeper insight into both individual and team performance.

Techniques such as 360-degree feedback, journaling, values assessment, and accountability plans can reveal hidden strengths, create lasting alignment, and promote a culture of continuous improvement. Integrate these tools into your everyday leadership practice to elevate your team's growth and success.

360-DEGREE FEEDBACK

You may have participated in someone else´s 360 feedback as a feedback giver, but if you have never experienced it before, 360-degree feedback is a process where you receive feedback about your performance from several sources. These sources can include your leader or direct supervisor, your peers, and the people you supervise. The term "360" indicates that the input comes from all around you, forming a full circle of perspectives, rather than just from one person at the top.

This kind of feedback is helpful because it shows how your behaviors and skills look to different people in different situations. You might learn about strengths you have not noticed, such as how effectively you communicate or how well you handle conflict. You can also discover areas that need work, such as time management or delegation. Many companies have a yearly, formal 360 feedback session, often organized by HR. During that session, participants fill out surveys or questionnaires, and their comments are then combined into a report for you to review.

However, you do not have to limit yourself to waiting for these official sessions. If you pay attention to everyday comments and conversations—with your teammates, your manager, or even your partners in other departments—you can spot patterns, learn what people appreciate, and take action on any issues right away. This ongoing, day-to-day approach lets you make small adjustments throughout the year, so you are always growing. By continuously seeking input from all angles, you give yourself the chance to get better at what you do and help your team perform at a higher level.

If your company does not run this officially you can gather it yourself.

1. Identify feedback givers – the process often starts by selecting a group of individuals (your lead, direct reports, peers, etc.) who regularly see you in action.

2. Data collection – those individuals fill out surveys or questionnaires, usually focusing on competencies like communication, collaboration, decision-making, or leadership style.
   Templates for these 360-Degree Feedbacking surveys are easily available online.

3. Anonymity and confidentiality – to encourage honesty, most 360 processes anonymize peer and direct-report feedback, so you see themes without identifying exactly who said what.

4. Consolidation and reporting – the results are then aggregated into a feedback report, highlighting patterns and themes—where you consistently excel and where there may be room for growth.

5. Review and action planning – you typically go over the report with a coach, HR professional, or your manager to interpret the results. From there, you create a personal development plan to build on your strengths and address any gaps.

JOURNALING EXERCISES

Keeping a journal is one of the most straightforward yet powerful ways to foster growth and self-awareness. By writing down thoughts, challenges, and progress each day or week, people gain clarity about what they are experiencing and why. This process can make it easier to spot recurring patterns or behaviors—both positive and negative—that might otherwise go unnoticed. For example, someone might realize they consistently struggle with time management on Mondays or notice that a quick midday break improves their afternoon productivity.

To make journaling an even richer experience, you can use specific prompts or questions. These might focus on problem-solving ("What was one challenge you faced and how did you address it?") or emotional well-being ("What moment today made you feel especially motivated—or particularly stressed?"). While the content of a journal is typically private, you and team members may choose to share key insights during one-on-ones or group reflections. Over time, those entries turn into a personalized record of growth, helping each person celebrate milestones, learn from setbacks, and stay engaged in their development. As a leader, you can use this yourself as well as encourage consistency for your team by reminding everyone how even brief, routine notes can spark meaningful realizations—and ultimately benefit both their individual success and the team's overall performance.

Reflect on what you have experienced today, this week or month.

VALUES ASSESSMENT

If you've never done a values assessment before, think of it as a way to uncover what truly drives you. By taking a moment to reflect on your core beliefs - maybe honesty, creativity, or teamwork - you give yourself a solid compass for both everyday decisions and bigger life choices. Once you know what matters most, your actions start to align with those values, and that can bring a real sense of purpose to your day. For a team, it means everyone is on the same page about why they do what they do, and work feels a lot more meaningful as a result.

Host a short workshop or meeting: Introduce the concept of a values assessment and explain why it matters. Let people know this is about finding out what personally motivates them, not judging anyone's beliefs.

Provide prompts. Offer simple, open-ended questions like "What do I believe in strongly at work?" or "What behaviors do I admire in others?" Ask each team member to list three to five values they hold dear.

Encourage reflection. Give everyone a few minutes of quiet time to jot down ideas. Emphasize honesty—this isn't about finding the "right" answer but about revealing what they truly care about.

Discuss as a group. Ask volunteers to share one or two core values and why they chose them. You might be surprised how these conversations can spark fresh insights and empathy.

Create alignment. As a team, identify how each person's values connect with the broader goals. You don't need perfect overlap, just an understanding that helps people see where they contribute best.

Follow up. Keep those values visible—maybe in a shared document or on a whiteboard. Check in during future one-on-ones or team huddles to see how everyone's values are guiding their work.

ACCOUNTABILITY PLANS

If you already know that you need an accountability plan for your team member, but are mainly struggling with the emotional aspects of starting that conversation, then go read chapter 8, about having those tough conversations. After that return here for the more "technical" tips.

As a new team lead, an accountability plan is a structured way to outline tasks, timelines, and goals for each person. It keeps everyone motivated and on track because it lays out a clear path to success. By having this plan, you reduce confusion about who does what, and everyone sees how their work connects to the bigger picture. It is a simple way to sharpen your team's focus and achieve meaningful results.

Start by clarifying the goal or deliverable you want to accomplish. Identify the tasks or milestones involved, and decide who is responsible for each step. Make sure everyone knows why their contribution matters, not just what they have to do. Set realistic deadlines so your team can pace themselves, and schedule regular progress updates to resolve any obstacles that arise. Use a shared spreadsheet or a project management app to track progress, and update the plan when priorities shift so everyone stays aligned. When a milestone is reached, take a moment to celebrate and discuss lessons learned, which helps build confidence for the next phase.

By creating an accountability plan, you provide your team with a clear roadmap showing exactly how each step leads to the final objective. Everyone knows what needs doing and by when, which cuts down on confusion and encourages genuine commitment. Without an accountability plan the person on your team is swimming blindly, a plan is what gives them structure and goals so they can actually feel they have something concrete to improve upon.

PART 4:
DEEPER INSIGHTS AND FRAMEWORKS

Having explored both fundamental and advanced coaching tools in the previous sections, you're now ready to dive into deeper insights and frameworks that can further elevate your leadership. This part focuses on techniques that address critical areas of team dynamics—everything from visualizing future success to managing energy levels and leveraging individual strengths. You'll also discover structured feedback frameworks to keep communication open and motivational interviewing approaches to guide hesitant team members toward meaningful change. Finally, we'll revisit the Eisenhower Matrix—this time applying it to help your team prioritize effectively.

These methods go beyond basic goal-setting or brainstorming. They're designed to sharpen your self-awareness as a leader, foster an environment of continuous learning, and make it easier for you to help your team tackle challenges head-on. Whether you choose to implement one or all of these frameworks, each tool offers a practical way to expand your coaching skill set and nurture a high-performing, resilient team.

VISUALIZATION TECHNIQUES

If you are leading a team for the first time, guiding them to picture their ideal future or a specific goal can ignite motivation and spark creative thinking. Encourage each person to imagine the outcome they want, describe it in detail, and note what steps or resources might be needed. Make time to discuss these visions together, in 1:1 meetings, so everyone feels invested in turning them into reality. Write down the shared picture and keep it where the team can easily and privately refer to it, whether in a digital workspace or on a whiteboard. Check in periodically to see how well each person is staying focused on that vision and whether any adjustments are necessary. By weaving visualization into your process, you help your team stay inspired and aligned as they move toward their objectives.

ENERGY MANAGEMENT

Pay close attention to everyone's physical, emotional, mental, and even spiritual energy levels. Encourage each person to note when they feel most alert or most drained, then discuss any patterns or challenges in one-on-ones or group settings. Share simple strategies, such as taking short breaks, stepping outside for fresh air, or switching tasks to recharge a tired mind. Remind your team that energy levels naturally rise and fall, so the goal is to find a balanced rhythm rather than maintain constant peak performance. When you see signs of fatigue or burnout, address them quickly by adjusting workloads, offering extra support, or guiding people to resources that can help. Bringing attention to these problems when they arise allows people to actually address them. In case you need to later part ways with a team member they will be grateful to have had a chance to turn things around. By being proactive about energy management, you keep productivity steady and create an environment where people can sustain their efforts in a healthy way.

FEEDBACK FRAMEWORKS (E.G., SBI MODEL)

Consider a structured approach like Situation-Behavior-Impact (SBI) for giving and receiving feedback. Start by describing the situation, point out the specific behavior you observed, and then explain the impact it had on the team or the outcome. For instance, you might say, "In yesterday's meeting, you suggested a new approach, which inspired the team to explore a different angle and ultimately speed up our planning process." Keep the feedback factual and concise, and allow time for the other person to respond. Encourage your team to use this model with each other so feedback stays clear and constructive instead of vague or confrontational. Over time, it builds trust and creates a culture where open communication can thrive.

Host a short workshop or meeting: Introduce the concept of a values assessment and explain why it matters. Let people know this is about finding out what personally motivates them, not judging anyone's beliefs.

Provide prompts. Offer simple, open-ended questions like "What do I believe in strongly at work?" or "What behaviors do I admire in others?" Ask each team member to list three to five values they hold dear.

Encourage reflection. Give everyone a few minutes of quiet time to jot down ideas. Emphasize honesty—this isn't about finding the "right" answer but about revealing what they truly care about.

Discuss as a group. Ask volunteers to share one or two core values and why they chose them. You might be surprised how these conversations can spark fresh insights and empathy.

Create alignment. As a team, identify how each person's values connect with the broader goals. You don't need perfect overlap, just an understanding that helps people see where they contribute best.

Follow up. Keep those values visible—maybe in a shared document or on a whiteboard. Check in during future one-on-ones or team huddles to see how everyone's values are guiding their work.

Situation

Behavior

Impact

Reflection

CLIFTONSTRENGTHS

CliftonStrengths assessment (previously known as StrengthsFinder), is a professional tool developed by Gallup that reveals the top talents a person naturally leans on. You complete it online by answering a series of questions, and then the system ranks your strongest qualities out of 34 possible themes. When you purchase access on the Gallup website, you usually receive a code to take the assessment and unlock a personalized report.

As a team lead, you might also coordinate a group session where a certified CliftonStrengths coach guides everyone through the process. Many coaches offer workshops that include both the assessment and follow-up discussions, allowing team members to share their results in a supportive setting. With expert facilitation, you gain deeper insights into how individual strengths can work together for a common goal.

Because the CliftonStrengths report highlights what each person does best, it becomes easier to assign tasks, form pairs, or build project teams around complementary skill sets. That can increase engagement and reduce burnout by making sure people spend more time where they truly excel. Over time, a strengths-based approach can lead to better collaboration and a healthier team culture.

MOTIVATIONAL INTERVIEWING (MI)

Motivational interviewing is a way to guide people who feel uncertain about making changes. Instead of directing them, you ask open-ended questions and reflect their answers, helping them discover why change might matter to them. By focusing on empathy and collaboration, you empower each person to tap into their own reasons for growth, which can lead to stronger commitment and better outcomes. Over time, this approach builds trust and makes it easier for everyone to discuss challenges and move forward together. A good book to learn more about motivational interviewing is "Motivational Interviewing: Helping People Change" by William R. Miller and Stephen Rollnick.

Example exercise for Motivational Interviewing:

1. Choose one team member who seems hesitant about a new project or workflow.
2. Ask, "What makes you feel unsure about this change?" and listen closely to their response.
3. Reflect back what you hear, for instance, "It sounds like you're worried about how this new process will affect your daily routine."
4. Explore possible benefits by asking, "What do you think could improve if we tried this new approach?"
5. Encourage them to decide on one small next step that feels manageable, such as testing a single part of the new process.
6. Follow up later to see how it went and offer support if they run into difficulties.

EISENHOWER MATRIX

Assist team members in using the Eisenhower Matrix to categorize tasks into urgent and important quadrants to better prioritize and manage time. Refer back to Chapter 2 part 1 on how to use the tool, but this time you are helping your team member who is struggling with their tasks to use it for prioritisation.

When coaching yourself or a team member, start by opening the Eisenhower Matrix together and asking which task feels both urgent and important right now. Use that first square to surface the stressor that is crowding everything else. Next, guide the person to sort the remaining work into the other three quadrants, pressing for honest answers about true deadlines and impact. This shared sorting turns a private swirl of worries into a visible map you can both examine. Once each task sits in a quadrant, agree on one immediate action for the urgent-important item, one scheduled block for the important-not-urgent work, one concise delegation note for anything urgent-not-important, and one bold line through whatever lands in the last box. End by revisiting the matrix at your next one-on-one to track progress and adjust priorities, showing the person how to use the tool as an ongoing self-coaching ritual rather than a one-time fix.

PART 5:
FOUR KEY COACHING APPROACHES

Active listening. Give your full attention when someone speaks. Pay close attention to their words, tone, and body language. Instead of thinking about your response while they're talking, focus on truly understanding their message. Show engagement by reflecting back what you hear—try saying, "It sounds like you're feeling uncertain about this project" to validate their perspective.

Asking powerful questions. Encourage deeper thinking with open-ended questions. Avoid yes-or-no prompts and instead ask, "What do you see as the biggest challenge here?" or "How would achieving this goal impact you?" These types of questions help team members uncover insights and find their own solutions.

Embracing silence. After asking a question or listening to someone's thoughts, don't rush to fill the silence. While it may feel uncomfortable, giving space allows for reflection and often leads to more thoughtful responses. Resist the urge to jump in—sometimes, the best insights come after a pause.

Keeping the conversation on track. Discussions can easily drift off-topic. If that happens, gently refocus by asking, "How does this connect to your main goal of...?" This keeps the conversation productive and aligned with their objectives.

PART 6:
THE ART OF POWERFUL QUESTIONING

Up to now, you've explored a wide range of coaching tools and frameworks that can elevate your leadership. But there's one skill that underpins them all: asking the right questions. The questions you pose can transform a routine check-in into a catalyst for self-discovery and long-term growth.

In this section, we'll delve deeper into why questioning matters, the qualities that make a question truly impactful, and practical examples you can use right away. By honing this ability, you'll help your team think more critically, take greater ownership of their actions, and find fresh solutions to complex problems—hallmarks of a thriving, empowered work environment.

Purpose of questions. Your questions should spark reflection, encourage problem-solving, and deepen self-awareness. Aim to guide rather than direct, helping team members clarify their thoughts and discover their own solutions. This empowers them and boosts their commitment to action.

Example: If someone is struggling with a task, instead of offering advice, ask, "What would success look like for you in this situation?"

Qualities of good coaching questions. Great questions are open-ended, clear, and non-judgmental. They prompt thought and avoid leading the person to a specific answer.

Example: Replace "Don't you think this approach is difficult?" with "What challenges do you foresee with this approach?"

Source of questions. Draw your questions from active listening and genuine curiosity. Let their words guide your inquiries. Reflecting their statements back to them shows you're engaged and encourages deeper exploration.

Example: If they say, "I'm overwhelmed," you might respond, "What factors are contributing to that feeling?"

EXAMPLES OF POWERFUL QUESTIONS

- For clarification: "What would achieving this goal mean for you?"
- To explore options: "What strategies have you considered so far?"
- To envision success: "Imagine you've overcome this hurdle—what steps did you take?"
- For accountability: "What actions will you commit to, and how can I support you?"
- To identify strengths: "Which of your strengths can you leverage here?"

These questions are designed to help team members reflect deeply and move forward confidently.

EXAMPLES OF OPEN COACHING QUESTIONS

For coaching you need open questions that cannot be answered with a simple yes or no. Here are some to guide you.

1. What do you see as the biggest obstacle in achieving your current goal, and how could you tackle it?
2. How would you describe your ideal outcome for this project, and what first step feels most realistic?
3. In what ways do you feel most supported when you face a challenging situation at work?
4. Why does this particular goal matter to you personally, and how might it connect to the team's objectives?
5. How do you usually approach tasks that feel overwhelming, and what could you try differently this time?
6. What strengths have you noticed in yourself that you haven't fully used yet?
7. Which past accomplishment makes you feel most confident, and why do you think it went so well?
8. How does your current workload align with your long-term career interests?
9. When you think about your day-to-day work, what one change would make things feel more manageable?
10. Why do you believe this project is important for the team's success, and how do you see yourself contributing?
11. How might you break down this larger challenge into smaller steps that are easier to handle?
12. What resources or support do you think you might need to move forward more effectively?
13. When you feel stressed, how do you usually respond, and what could help you find a better balance?
14. Why do you think you've been hesitant to take the next step, and what would make you feel ready?

15. How could you adjust your routine to make more time for focused, high-impact work?

16. What do you hope to learn about yourself by taking on this new responsibility?

17. How have you overcome similar obstacles in the past, and what can you apply to this situation?

18. Why do you think communication in our team might be falling short, and how could we improve it?

19. How do you picture success once this project wraps up, and who might you want to recognize or involve?

20. Which area of your current role feels most exciting to you, and how can you build on that energy?

21. How might someone else approach this challenge differently, and what could you learn from that perspective?

22. What would it look like if you fully embraced the changes we're discussing, and how would it help your growth?

23. Which small victory could you celebrate right now that might give you momentum for the bigger tasks ahead?

24. Why do you feel this particular task is blocking your progress, and how could you see it in a more positive light?

25. How do you think the team's culture affects your motivation, and what would you like to shift, if anything?

26. In what ways could collaboration with another teammate lighten your load or spark new ideas?

27. What makes you proud of the work you've done lately, and how could you deepen that sense of accomplishment?

28. How can you reorganize your priorities so the most important tasks receive the attention they deserve?

29. What would happen if you took a small risk in your approach to this project, and how might that change the outcome?

30. When you reflect on your recent challenges, what common threads do you see, and how can you address them?

What you've just read may feel like a lot to take in: because it is! Don't worry. Start small by picking one tool or approach that resonates with you most, and practice it until you feel comfortable.

Then, add another. By embracing coaching as a leadership tool, you're not only enhancing your team's skills, you're transforming the entire work environment. With a focus on empowerment, active listening, and powerful questioning, you'll foster growth, innovation, and success. Integrate these coaching techniques gradually, and watch both your team, and yourself, thrive.

EXERCISE: TURNING CLOSED QUESTIONS INTO OPEN ONES

Below is a two-column activity for the workbook. read each yes-or-no question on the left, then rewrite it as an open question in the blank space on the right. aim for wording that invites detail and reflection.

Closed Questions	Your Open Question
Did you finish the task?	
Are you happy with your progress?	
Is this approach working?	
Are you worried about the deadline?	
Do you need help?	
Do you understand the goal?	
Is the project on track?	
Do you agree with the decision?	
Is the timeline realistic?	
Did you get feedback from the team?	
Is the next step clear?	
Is this the best solution?	

Tip: if you get stuck, start with "what," "how," or "in what ways" to keep the question open

CHAPTER 7:
HIRING, ONBOARDING, AND DEVELOPING YOUR TEAM

As a new leader, hiring the right people is often one of your responsibilities. The team you build will shape your ability to reach goals, influence the culture, and drive long-term success. Before posting that job ad, remember—hiring is a major investment. Consider all options, including temporary workers or consultants, to ensure expanding your team is the right move.

Once you decide to hire, the work doesn't stop there. Bringing someone on board is just the first step. Effective onboarding and ongoing development are what truly set new hires—and your entire team—up for success.

PART 1:
HIRING THE RIGHT PEOPLE

As a new leader, hiring the right people is often one of your responsibilities. The team you build will shape your ability to reach goals, influence the culture, and drive long-term success. Before posting that job ad, remember—hiring is a major investment. Consider all options, including temporary workers or consultants, to ensure expanding your team is the right move.

Once you decide to hire, the work doesn't stop there. Bringing someone on board is just the first step. Effective onboarding and ongoing development are what truly set new hires—and your entire team—up for success.

Hiring at the right time helps maintain efficiency and achieve organizational goals. Make sure you have access to relevant information related to the growth of the company so you can take timely action. Because if you need to hire specialists, hiring is rarely a fast process; it may take you months to find the right person.

If the company does not have a clear hiring plan, there are some signs that might indicate it's time to expand:

- If your team is overburdened and consistently missing deadlines, making errors, or showing signs of burnout, it may mean you don't have enough resources to manage the workload.
- If you lack specific expertise needed for an upcoming project or initiative, hiring a specialist or outsourcing a consultant can fill that void and boost your team's capabilities.
- If your organization is expanding, proactive hiring can help you meet future demands without overworking existing staff.

Before hiring, you need to assess whether adding a new member is truly necessary. Here are a few questions you should answer before going forward:

- Do we have the capacity to meet goals?
- Do we have enough people to handle current and future objectives with our existing team?
- Is this increased workload just a short-term spike, or does it indicate consistent growth?
- Can we reorganize, delegate, automate, or outsource the work instead of hiring someone new?

Crafting the ideal candidate profile is key to attracting people who have the right skills and fit into your team's culture.

Steps to create a strong candidate profile:

- Define the role. Clearly write out responsibilities, specific duties, goals, and expectations. Explain in detail how the new position supports your team and contributes to broader organizational objectives.
- Identify key skills and qualities your new team member must have by making simple lists of:
    o Most important technical skills they can't succeed without or you don't have time to teach (e.g., basic computer skills, languages).
    o Soft skills the new member has to have, like communication, teamwork, and problem-solving.
    o Personal traits that align with your team's values, such as adaptability, initiative, or resilience. There is an old saying that you can be taught everything but not personality. So choose well.
- Specify success indicators. Short-term goals define what success looks like in the first 30, 60, and 90 days. Long-term objectives define what you expect them to achieve within the first year.
- Understand team dynamics. Sometimes cultural fit and personality are some of the most important factors to consider in the talent pool. If you have a very tight team that has to deal with a lot of pressure and be flexible, an unyielding talent who works better in a set environment could cause the collapse of the entire team.
- Work closely with HR or hiring specialists to ensure the process runs smoothly and follows organizational and legal guidelines. Establish realistic deadlines based on urgency and organizational priorities. Keep in touch throughout the hiring process to answer questions and ensure alignment at each step.

Conducting effective interviews is about discovering how well the candidate matches the ideal profile you have established. Keep in mind that the "ideal" candidate might be impossible to find, so you will likely have to choose who fits best from available talent.

How to prepare for the interview:

- Develop a set of standardized questions that allows you to evaluate all candidates in a fair and objective way.
- Focus on practical skills by incorporating scenario-based questions or problem-solving exercises that reflect real challenges the role will face. Example: "Could you walk me through a tough project you handled?"
- Assess cultural fit by asking about communication preferences, work styles, and how they handle teamwork or conflict. Example: "What type of team environment helps you perform at your best?"
- Look beyond experience by considering potential and attitude just as seriously as past achievements—sometimes motivation and willingness to learn can outweigh limited experience. Example: "How have you approached learning new skills or tackling unfamiliar challenges?"

Carefully chosen questions reveal if someone truly fits your team. Open-ended, coaching-style prompts often show far more than yes-or-no queries. They encourage the candidate to think out loud, show their reasoning, and expose genuine capabilities or shortcomings. Avoid rushing in to clarify or help them improve their answer—this is the moment to see how they cope on their own, not a coaching session. If they struggle or offer a weak response, let them sit with that discomfort instead of rescuing them. Only after you decide to bring them on board should you shift into teaching and guiding mode. Until then, your role is to assess what they can do under pressure and whether they can truly meet the demands of the role.

Ask yourself:

What is one role on your current (or future) team that you feel needs the most attention right

now? How would you describe the must-have skills for it?

EXERCISE: CRAFT YOUR CANDIDATE PROFILE

Write a draft "Ideal Candidate Profile" for a position you need (or want) to fill.This will give you a concrete yardstick for judging applicants rather than relying on charisma during interviews.

- Write one or two sentences to explain why the position exists and how it supports team goals.
- Focus on what a successful hire must deliver in daily work.
- Ask yourself which abilities would take too long to teach and note only those that are truly non-negotiable.
- Think about the behaviours your company culture values most : such as clear communication, adaptability, or proactive problem solving.
- Combine the points into a short paragraph you can share with HR or hiring partners.
- Sanity-check with a peer or your own lead.
- Ask whether a person meeting this profile would move your goals forward and adjust if needed.

Role mission:	
Core responsibilities	1. 2. 3.
Essential technical skills	• • •
Top soft skills	1. 2. 3.
Success indicators	30 days: 60 days: 90 days: 1 year:

PART 2:
ONBOARDING NEW HIRES

Onboarding shapes how new hires experience your team and company from day one. It shows them they're valued, helps them build confidence through clear guidance and early wins, and increases long-term retention by making them feel supported and connected.

I have firsthand experience with seeing how powerful proper onboarding can be. It will completely change how fast new hires become loyal and motivated workers. Believe me, people want and need to know how they could be productive faster. I haven't met a good hire who wanted to be a dead-weight in my life and I have seen thousands. People are acting up only because of being confused or being in the wrong place at the wrong time and that is something why hiring has to be good.

WHAT WE SUGGEST TO HAVE FOR SUCCESSFUL ONBOARDING:

- Clear roadmap that consists of 30-, 60-, and 90-day realistic goals so new hires know what to focus on.
- Pair the new hire with a mentor from the team who can offer guidance and help them adjust.
- Make a proper cultural introduction by explaining team values, processes, and communication norms upfront.
- Offer regular check-ins by meeting weekly to offer feedback, answer questions, and track progress.
- Encourage connections by allowing shadowing, cross-department introductions, and small collaborative projects to help them build relationships early on.

PART 3:
DEVELOPING YOUR TEAM

Welcoming a new hire is just the beginning. What truly builds a high-performing, loyal team is what comes next—training, support, and continuous development. But before diving into how to develop your people, there's one core principle:

There are no fixed rules.

At least, not rules you can apply the same way to every person or organization. Instead, there are guidelines—and those depend on your company's structure, leadership style, budget, and, most importantly, the people you're working with.

Before you train anyone, stop and consider:

- What does success look like in this role?
- What are this person's learning preferences and motivations?
- What resources are realistically available to support their growth?

Every person learns differently. Every topic may require a different approach. And every organization is unique. There are thousands of ready-made training options, from one-off workshops to long-term courses. You can hire external trainers or craft your own development plans from scratch. Whichever path you choose, remember: these are your people, and this is your responsibility.

If you have time to experiment, test, and iterate, great. But if you need to move quickly and minimize costly mistakes, you'll need a systematic approach: planning with intention, accounting for variables, and building frameworks that are both structured and flexible.

THINK IN TWO LAYERS: STRATEGY AND PLANS

A highly effective way to approach team development is by separating the long-term strategy from the short-term plans.

- Strategy is your big-picture vision. It should be flexible enough to adapt as your company grows, yet stable enough to provide direction for at least a year. Constantly changing strategy creates confusion. Changing it mid-year can be even more disruptive. That's why your development strategy should include alternate paths, contingency options, and enough room to grow or scale back if needed.

- Plans, on the other hand, are short-term and action-oriented. These can be weekly, monthly, or quarterly, depending on your needs. Good plans align with your strategy and ensure steady progress. They cut down on rework, prevent burnout, and give clarity to both managers and employees.

The two work together:

- A strategy without plans is just a dream.
- Plans without a strategy lead to aimless busywork.

When done right, this layered approach ensures your development efforts are both well-coordinated and resilient—even if you're rapidly hiring or pivoting your business model.

WHY DEVELOPMENT MATTERS

- People are more likely to stay when they see a clear path for growth.
- Continuous skill-building leads to higher productivity and stronger performance.
- A learning culture encourages creativity, openness, and better problem-solving.

HOW TO SUPPORT DEVELOPMENT

Set clear personal and professional targets with each team member. Goals should feel relevant and motivating.

Offer meaningful growth opportunities—through training, cross-functional projects, or mentorship.

Give regular, constructive feedback that helps people understand both their strengths and areas for improvement.

Celebrate milestones and achievements, big or small, to drive engagement and consistency.

EXERCISE: CREATING A COLLABORATIVE DEVELOPMENT PLAN

1. Choose one person on your team who's open to growth or shows potential in a certain area.
2. Have a conversation with them about a key skill or area of growth they'd like to focus on—something that will boost both their performance and motivation.
3. Decide together on one or two actions or trainings to address this skill (e.g., job-shadowing, online courses, new project responsibilities).
4. Agree on a timeline or milestones, ensuring it fits their role and workload.
5. Plan a simple feedback process (quick check-ins, regular debriefs) and discuss how you'll recognize any progress or achievements.

This approach keeps the team member involved in every step, promoting ownership of their development and ensuring the plan is mutually beneficial.

PART 4:
BUDGETING FOR HIRING, TRAINING, AND RETENTION

Managing your budget effectively is crucial for making smart hires, delivering quality training, and retaining valuable talent. It's crucial to balance your available budget, the caliber of potential hires, the cost of training, and the long-term return on investment.

Paying for experience vs. potential: If your budget is tight, consider hiring someone who shows promise but needs development. Make sure you allocate enough funds for their training and onboarding. If you can afford more experienced professionals, you'll likely spend less time on training, but the higher salary should pay off in speed and quality of output.

- If funds are limited, focus on candidates with potential and craft a robust training plan.
- If budget allows, consider someone with proven experience who can deliver immediate results.

Managing budget vs. turnover:

- The cost of high turnover adds up. Constant hiring and training can quickly become expensive, even if you pay lower salaries upfront.
- If wages are low, people might leave as soon as a better-paying opportunity comes along. In such cases, development opportunities alone might not be enough to retain them if they're struggling financially.

Finding the balance:

- If turnover is high and wages are too low, reevaluate your pay structure. Training alone won't compensate for an unlivable wage.
- If turnover is high but you can raise salaries, offering more competitive compensation helps retain talent long enough for you to recoup hiring and training costs.
- If you can't afford seasoned talent, invest in mentorship,

structured learning pathways, and clear career progression.

- There's always an option to use temporary help from specialists.

High turnover can negate any short-term savings from lower wages. Recruiting, training, and lost productivity can exceed the cost of offering a better salary from the start. When you retain people longer, they grow more efficient, improve team morale, and boost overall productivity, all of which positively impacts your bottom line.

PART 5:
HOW MUCH IS TURNOVER COSTING YOU?

Look at your team's turnover rate (or best estimate). How much time and money have you spent replacing, onboarding, and training new hires in the past year? You may be able to get all these numbers from your own lead or HR, if not we have outlined briefly on how to calculate this.

Here's a smart way to ask your colleague for these numbers in an email: *"I'm mapping out a quick turnover-cost snapshot to guide our upcoming hiring and retention plan. Could you send me last year's head-count numbers along with your best estimates for per-hire recruiting, onboarding, and training costs? Even rough figures will let me calculate our turnover rate, size the total spend, and identify the smartest places to save. Thanks for your help—this data will keep our budget discussion grounded in facts."*

This helps you see the full hidden price of losing people so you can make smarter hiring and retention choices.

STEP-BY-STEP INSTRUCTIONS

1. Gather basic numbers. Write down how many employees were on your team at the start of last year and how many left during the year.

2. Calculate your turnover rate. Use the simple formula: departures ÷ average head-count × 100. If head-count started at ten and three people left, turnover is $3 \div 10 \times 100 = 30$ percent.

3. Estimate recruiting costs per hire. Include job-board fees, recruiter commissions, and the hours you or HR spent reviewing résumés and interviewing. Put in a best-guess figure if you lack exact data.

4. Estimate onboarding costs per hire. Count the new hire's salary during ramp-up, the mentor's time, and any equipment or licences issued.

5. Estimate training costs per hire. Add course fees, conference tickets, or internal workshop hours.

6. Multiply. Take the sums from steps 3-5, add them together, and multiply by the number of people you replaced last year.

7. Fill in the turnover snapshot table below.

8. Identify high-cost areas. Circle the line that surprised you most and jot one idea to reduce or recoup that cost in the coming year.

9. Share insights. Summarise your findings in a short email or slide for your manager so budgeting talks are grounded in real numbers.

Here is a simple one to give you an idea:

	Per-Hire Cost (estimate)	Number Of Replacements	Total Cost
Recruiting			
Onboarding			
Training			
Grand total			

Ask yourself:

- Does your turnover rate feel sustainable for the team's workload and morale?
- Which single change—better screening, clearer onboarding, pay adjustment—might cut the total cost quickest?

If you have zero hard data, use a conservative placeholder that fits your industry average (for example, 30 percent of annual salary per hire) rather than skipping the calculation; a rough figure is more useful than none at all.

CHAPTER 8:
NAVIGATING THE TOUGHEST MOMENTS

A note before proceeding: The information in this book, especially this chapter, provide only general guidance and is not legal advice. Always consult your Human Resources department or legal counsel for specific procedures and obligations in your jurisdiction.

PART 1:
GENERAL GUIDELINES FOR LETTING SOMEONE GO

If you have jumped ahead to this chapter without fully exploring the sections on setting expectations, running meaningful one on ones, or defining success metrics, you may find less tactical support for what you are facing. Still, if you are here because you are in a difficult situation right now, read on. Keep in mind that future hires and current team members benefit most when clear foundations are laid from the start. With role clarity, open feedback, and a shared understanding of success, the need for termination becomes increasingly rare.

Letting someone go is arguably one of the hardest responsibilities in leadership. It is not just the delivery of tough news; it is also the complex reality of addressing performance or cultural misalignment with care, respect, and accountability. Ideally, no termination comes as a surprise. When you have consistently communicated expectations, offered honest feedback, and provided opportunities for improvement, parting ways becomes a matter of alignment rather than punishment.

Preparing for this kind of conversation matters. Relying on impulse or intuition alone can lead to a rushed and insensitive process. You need to understand precisely why the decision is being made, ensure you are following fair processes, and be prepared to communicate the reasons calmly and compassionately. Written documentation and a review of relevant policies help ground the discussion in clarity rather than emotion. It is possible to handle these moments in a way that maintains dignity for all involved.

You might reflect on these questions before finalizing the decision:

- Have you given the individual a fair chance to improve?
- Is there clear documentation that demonstrates why this role is no longer a fit?
- Have you laid out the conversation in your mind so you can deliver it with empathy and clarity?

A well conducted termination acknowledges a mismatch between the individual's current role and the organization's needs. By framing it this way, you can keep the focus on alignment rather than personal failure, and where feasible, offer transitional support such as severance, references, or guidance. This approach helps the person maintain self respect and, whenever possible, opens a path toward a better suited opportunity.

It is also important to remember that once the individual leaves, the rest of the team will have questions. They will want to know how this happened, why it happened, and what it means for them. Offer reassurance that the decision was not made abruptly or unfairly. Emphasize your commitment to transparency, feedback, and fairness. Acknowledge the emotional toll that losing a colleague can bring, especially if strong personal connections existed. Quiet, one on one conversations may help individuals process the change. Trust can remain intact (or even strengthen) when your team senses genuine thoughtfulness and honesty in how you communicate the situation.

Though firing someone should never feel easy (if it does, something deeper is amiss) the lingering discomfort indicates empathy and genuine concern. With a clear, calm, and compassionate mindset, you can address these moments with integrity, aiming for a parting that still affirms the individual's value. The ultimate goal is to ensure they leave with self respect and a sense that they can thrive elsewhere, even if this particular role was not the right fit.

On a personal note, I understand how overwhelming this can be. Early in my career, I found myself in environments where poor hires happened too often, each one taking a significant emotional toll. My perspective began to shift after reading Patty McCord's Powerful: Building a Culture of Freedom and Responsibility and later hearing her speak in person. Her insights transformed how I approach both hiring and letting people go. If you have not already, I suggest exploring her work. It may offer a fresh perspective on handling these challenging moments.

> You might pause here for another moment of reflection
> - How do you feel about your own communication style when delivering hard news?
> - What kind of support system or resources do you have as you navigate these decisions?
> - How might you use this experience to reinforce healthier communication and clearer expectations across your team?
>
> These questions can guide you in processing the emotional weight and practical details of letting someone go. Although it will never be simple, you can handle it with compassion, respect, and a sense of accountability that fosters trust in your leadership long after the conversation ends.

PART 2:
TURNING CHALLENGES INTO LEARNING OPPORTUNITIES

Postmortems are some of the most valuable tools in a leader's toolkit, yet they are often underused or misunderstood. These structured reflections help teams examine what happened during a project, decision, or process, especially when things didn't go as planned. They are not about assigning blame; they are about learning and moving forward with clarity.

Reflection. "Think of a recent challenge your team faced. How might a postmortem have helped you understand what went wrong?"

By reviewing challenges—whether it is a missed deadline, a failed project, or a difficult personnel decision—you create a space for growth. Postmortems turn setbacks into opportunities for reflection, improvement, and better decision making. They encourage open communication and reinforce a team culture where continuous learning is expected and supported.

Reflection. "Which aspects of postmortems (reflection, improvement, decision making) resonate most with your current leadership challenges?"

Postmortems can be used in a wide range of scenarios:
- When a deadline is missed, they help clarify whether the timeline was realistic, if resources were adequate, or whether priorities got off track.
- After a project fails, they reveal gaps in scope, planning, or collaboration.
- In the aftermath of a crisis or emergency, they highlight how the team responded and what protocols need strengthening.
- Even following the termination of a team member, they allow you to consider whether warning signs were overlooked or if earlier interventions might have helped.
- When a process breaks down, they help uncover inefficiencies or misaligned responsibilities.

When used thoughtfully, postmortems drive growth rather than guilt. They sharpen your leadership, help your team course correct, and build resilience over time.

> Reflection. "Identify which scenario (missed deadline, failed project, crisis, personnel issue, process breakdown) you or your team encountered most recently. What was your immediate response, and how might it have been different if you had conducted a postmortem?"

To run one effectively, start with the facts. Map out what happened and when. Stay objective, focusing first on the timeline and events before jumping into interpretations. Then gather the people involved and create a psychologically safe space for honest feedback. Ask direct but open questions: What went well? What did not? Why? What could we do differently next time?

> Reflection. "When inviting participants, how will you ensure everyone feels safe enough to speak honestly?"

Once insights emerge, turn them into action. Document the lessons learned and build a clear follow-up plan with specific responsibilities and timelines. Keep an eye on progress and be ready to adapt if new challenges surface. The goal is not perfection, but improvement.

As you integrate postmortems into your leadership routine, stay focused on constructive feedback and practical outcomes. Celebrate what worked, learn from what did not, encourage participation, and normalize these conversations as part of your team's rhythm. When done consistently and respectfully, postmortems become a force for lasting improvement.

> Reflection. "What steps can you take immediately to show your team that postmortem findings will lead to real changes?"

Leadership is not about avoiding mistakes, but about growing through them. A successful postmortem reinforces trust, strengthens team cohesion, and helps you lead with greater clarity and confidence. Embrace these moments and you will build a team and a culture that is equipped to thrive through whatever comes next.

> Reflection. "Looking ahead, how do you plan to incorporate postmortems into your regular leadership cadence? What is one commitment you can make right now?"

STEP-BY STEP GUIDE ON OF HOW TO RUN A MEANINGFUL POST-MORTEM

1. PREPARE THE GROUNDWORK

Start by building a neutral picture of what happened. Collect the key dates, deadlines, and milestones in order, note everyone who took part or was affected, and write a short line on what you hoped would happen versus what actually occurred. Having these facts on one page lets every participant begin the meeting from the same place and keeps opinions from crowding out evidence.

Reflection Questions

- What data or evidence do you typically overlook when evaluating a recent project or incident?
- How can you ensure that everyone involved agrees on the basic facts before the meeting?

Quick checklist

- Timeline: list events in the order they happened.
- People: record who was involved or impacted.
- Goals versus results: write the intended outcome beside the real one.

2. INVITE THE RIGHT PEOPLE

Choose attendees with care. Include the people who worked on the project, those who approved key decisions, and anyone clearly affected by the outcome, but keep the group small enough for real dialogue—five to eight is usually plenty. When you send the invite, add a single line that frames the meeting as a learning session, not a blame session, so everyone feels safe to speak. Before you hit send, scan the list once more and ask yourself whether a useful voice is missing—perhaps someone from support, finance, or another team who saw the impact from a different angle.

Reflection Question

- Which viewpoint do you tend to forget to include, and how will you make sure it is represented next time?

Quick Checklist

- Draft the attendee list and highlight the must-have voices.
- Add a "we are here to learn, not to blame" sentence to the calendar invite.
- Check for overlooked perspectives and adjust the list if needed.

3. GUIDE THE CONVERSATION

Steer the discussion with a few broad, curious questions, then give people time to think. Begin with "What worked better than expected?" move to "Where did we struggle and why?" and finish with "What will we try differently next time?" Resist the urge to fill every pause; silent moments often surface the most useful insights. As you listen, watch for patterns and unspoken assumptions—all clues to the real root causes.

Reflection Questions

- Which question tends to generate the most revealing responses in your team meetings?

- How comfortable are you with silence when waiting for people to think and respond?

Quick Checklist

- Draft three open questions that touch success, shortfalls, and future fixes.
- Promise yourself you will wait at least five seconds after each question before speaking again.
- List any hot-button topics in advance and plan neutral wording so feedback stays constructive.

4. CAPTURE AND SHARE INSIGHTS

Capture the lessons while they are fresh. First, name one person the scribe who types key points into a shared document as the meeting unfolds. Second, within twenty-four hours, tighten those raw notes into a short paragraph that explains what happened, why it happened, and what will change next time. Third, save the summary in a place every team member can reach, such as the project folder or a shared drive, and send a link to anyone who needs the information for future work.

Reflection Questions

- How do you typically record decisions and insights in meetings?
- Where will you store this information so it does not get lost or forgotten?

Quick Checklist

- Assign a scribe to capture major themes on a shared document.
- After the meeting, condense the main points into a single, concise paragraph or bulleted list.
- Decide where the summary will live (e.g., a shared drive, project management tool) and who needs to see it.

5. TURN REFLECTION INTO ACTION

Turn insights into commitments your team can see and track. First write one clear action for each lesson, second name the person who owns that action, and third set a realistic deadline. Enter these three pieces of information in a simple table with columns for Action, Owner, and Deadline, then sort the rows by urgency so the most critical items rise to the top. Send the table to the group, add it to your usual project tracker, and review it in every status meeting until each line is marked complete.

Reflection Questions

- What is one concrete change you can make immediately?
- How will you hold people (including yourself) accountable for completing these next steps?

Quick Checklist

- Create a table with three columns labeled "Action," "Owner," and "Deadline."
- Rank the actions by importance or urgency.
- Decide how you will inform the broader team of these next steps and track their progress.

6. CHECK IN AND ADAPT

Keep the action plan alive after the meeting. Set a recurring calendar invite—weekly for urgent fixes or every other week for routine items—and use that slot to ask whether each task is underway, on track, or blocked. Agree on one or two simple signs of success for every action, such as a reduced error rate or a faster response time, and note those measures alongside the task. When a step is not delivering the expected result, record what you learned, adjust the approach, and set a new deadline. Repeat this review cycle until every item is either completed or replaced by a better solution.

Reflection Questions

- How often will you schedule check-ins to discuss progress on postmortem action items?
- What metrics or signs will tell you if improvements are working?

Quick Checklist

- Set a recurring calendar invite (weekly or biweekly) to review the action plan.
- Define how you will measure whether each action item is making a positive impact.
- If you discover that a solution is not working as expected, document why and propose adjustments.

It's all rather simple:

Start by collecting a neutral timeline of what happened. Invite just the people who shaped or felt the impact so the discussion stays focused. Ask open questions, listen without blame, and note the real lessons. Turn each lesson into an action with a clear owner and deadline, then review the list at regular check-ins and adjust as needed. Working this simple loop—facts, voices, questions, lessons, action, follow-up—turns every post-mortem into steady progress and helps the team grow stronger after each setback.

CHAPTER 9:
NURTURING YOUR WELL-BEING

Stepping into a leadership role, whether you are brand new or have just started, comes with both excitement and pressure. You have energy and enthusiasm for what is possible, but you can also feel pulled in a thousand directions. It is at this stage that caring for your mental well being is not just a nice to have; it is essential.

In my own experience, the real challenge was not leadership itself; it was my inability to say no and to set healthy limits. I was so eager to prove myself and help everyone that I rarely paused to consider how much I was taking on. That constant over extension eventually led to burnout. If you have not yet read about saying no (see Chapter 6), now is a good time: learning how to refuse extra demands, or at least negotiate timelines, can be one of your strongest tools for protecting your mental health and maintaining your motivation over the long haul.

A strong foundation for mental wellness starts with self awareness. Ask yourself: What helps me recharge? What are my personal non negotiables? These might be activities like exercise, reading, alone time, or family dinners. Whatever they are, treat them seriously. Block them into your calendar so you are reminded to step away, rest, or say no to extra meetings when necessary.

Being well is not just about scheduling breaks, though. It is also about designing your day with intention. Take a moment to review your calendar: Are you leaving room for deep work, collaboration, and rest? Or are you letting nonstop notifications and back to back meetings dictate your day? The productivity tactics in Chapter 3, such as time blocking and do not disturb settings, can help you reclaim your focus.

Communication also plays a huge role. If your workload feels unmanageable, tell your manager or lead. Explain that by honoring your well being, you can show up more productively and with greater clarity. The same principle applies at home: let loved ones know when you need dedicated downtime or quiet space to reset.

Emotional resilience is another key part of the puzzle. Make a habit of checking in with yourself. That can be as simple as reflecting each evening: What challenged me today? How did I respond? What am I grateful for? Building these small moments of reflection can help you process the highs and lows of leadership without letting stress quietly build.

Burnout does not always show up dramatically. Often, it is subtle, like a creeping loss of motivation, moodiness, or constant fatigue. Pay attention to those signals. If you start to sense the pressure becoming too great, do not wait. Speak with a coach or therapist, or confide in a trusted colleague. Seeking support early is far better than hitting a breaking point.

Finally, remember that resilience, like leadership itself, is something you develop over time. Connect with your deeper sense of purpose: Why did I step into this role? What excites me about it? Celebrate small wins, and remind yourself that perfection is not required; sustainability is. By modeling healthy boundaries and self care, you will also create a more open, supportive environment for your team. You show them that leadership does not have to come at the cost of well being. In fact, the best leadership is sustained by it.

EXERCISE: MENTAL WELL BEING CHECK IN

Take about 15 minutes this evening or during your next break to reflect on the following:

1. Recall one recent moment when you felt overwhelmed. What triggered it, and how did you respond?
2. List three activities that genuinely help you recharge. How often are you actually doing them?
3. Identify one small boundary you can set this week to protect your time or energy.
4. Write a short intention that supports your well being. For example: "Tomorrow, I will take a full lunch break without checking emails."

Repeat this check in weekly. Leadership is not about pushing yourself at all costs; it is about showing up with the clarity, energy, and care that let both you and your team thrive.

CHAPTER 10:
"JUST DO IT"– PROGRESS OVER PERFECTION

As you come to the final chapter of this workbook, take a moment to pause and reflect on your leadership journey so far. You have learned that effective leadership involves not only clear communication and strategic planning but also a willingness to learn from experience. In this chapter, we explore the idea that progress, even if imperfect, is far more valuable than waiting for a flawless outcome. Many new leaders feel compelled to deliver finished work every time, but history shows that great ideas grow through collaboration and refinement. While my co-author has found that sharing early drafts can spark innovative discussions, I understand the hesitation that comes from presenting work that does not yet meet your highest standards. The purpose of this chapter is to remind you that while excellence is the ultimate goal, the process of getting there happens one step at a time. Use these pages as an opportunity to shift your focus from chasing perfection to celebrating progress.

Imagine a new performance review template for your team. Rather than waiting until every detail is immaculate, consider sharing a rough version with a trusted colleague or mentor. Ask for feedback on whether the format is clear and if the questions address the team's real needs. By showing your work in progress, you invite constructive input that can refine your ideas and help you avoid spending too much time on perfecting every aspect before you have the chance to iterate.

In practice, this often means setting clear, essential standards for accuracy, safety, or compliance while accepting that other parts of your plan will evolve through iterative feedback. Producing deliverables that are solid enough to stand on their own, yet flexible enough to integrate suggestions, allows you to move forward while still maintaining quality. As a leader, you set the tone for your team. When you openly share a first draft with a few trusted individuals, you encourage an environment where collaborative feedback is not only welcomed but expected. This does not mean you settle for less than the best; it means you trust your judgment enough to embrace the learning process and refine your work as real feedback comes in.

Remember that perfection is an ideal, not a practical standard. The real challenge lies in taking decisive action despite uncertainties and imperfections. If you hold out for the perfect solution, you may never move forward. Instead, celebrating progress—no matter how incremental—fosters a culture where mistakes are seen as learning opportunities rather than failures. Your goal is to maintain a high standard for final outcomes while remaining open to change and improvement along the way.

REFLECTION EXERCISE

Take a few minutes now to consider a project you have been hesitating to share or finalize. Ask yourself:

- What small imperfections can I accept in this draft if it means I will get valuable feedback?
- How might early input help transform a good idea into a great one?

Write down your thoughts and note one specific area where you can release a work-in-progress version to a trusted peer. Let this be a stepping stone toward a more resilient final product.

When you step away from these pages, commit to taking immediate, tangible action. Revisit a lingering project or idea and share it as a work in progress. Gather honest feedback and use it to refine your approach, always remembering that each iteration brings you closer to your vision. In a world filled with competing opinions, your task is to filter through the noise and trust your judgment enough to keep moving forward. Embrace progress over perfection and let continuous improvement be the hallmark of your leadership style.

ABOUT THE AUTHORS

Helen Maidre is a chief executive with a rare ability to combine human-centered leadership with the precision required in tightly regulated fields. She is both practitioner and thinker: a CEO who runs production and quality systems, and a mentor who turns fuzzy ideals into practical skills. Her professional backbone formed in international high-growth environments. At Wise (formerly TransferWise) she was an early shaper of customer support for a rapidly expanding service and built top-tier teams. As CEO of PropsAid.eu she leads the development and manufacturing of ultra-realistic trauma training tools for the healthcare and crisis-training market, and with her team has taken part in the HFE accelerator. As a founder she has also contributed to educational audiovisual content at the video production company Must Post.

Her experience has a strong Japan chapter. With the GIG-A founding team in Tokyo she built a customer support organization from the ground up, adapted global ways of working to the Japanese market, brought departmental processes to ISO 9001 standards, and shaped a team that performed under high expectations in a different work culture. This taught Helen to translate vision into precise routines, coach the team to prioritize, and build systems that hold under pressure.

Her motivation runs deeper than business goals. At 36 Helen returned to university to study health because she wanted to do more for the well-being of people in Estonia. She believes workplace leadership culture is an important public-health lever. Clarity, fairness, and a sense of safety at work reduce stress, help prevent burnout, and create conditions where people can truly do their best work. This book aims to lift leadership culture in Estonia, especially for new managers at the start of their journey.

Helen Paas is a strategic operator who has built training systems from scratch in several companies, led global teams of trainers and mentors for years, and helped hundreds of new hires ramp up quickly. As Global Head of Training at Wise (formerly TransferWise) she was responsible for the training function across multiple locations in Budapest, Tallinn, and Tampa, led her international team, and supported units in Asia. Her focus covered the development paths of more than 600 agents and over 50 managers, as well as the effective onboarding of 30 to 60 new employees each month.

Helen is an accomplished planner. She coordinated training across two continents and two functions, Customer Support and Compliance, and was one of the creators and implementers of the company-wide onboarding program. Her work rests on the belief that good leadership culture can be learned. With the right tools, concrete feedback, and clear boundaries any team can move toward success with a steady compass.

As a coach Helen believes in developing potential through practical skills. She holds an international coach credential from Erickson Academy and has completed extensive advanced training in systematic training management and service operations. She applies the principles of the COPC CX standard, an international performance-management framework for customer experience and contact centers, which helps establish a clear goal tree, a consistent KPI system, and quality routines.

In this handbook Helen Paas shares the core of the techniques and tools she has tested many times in real life. She hopes this shared experience helps each reader begin a new leadership role wisely, effectively, and perhaps a little more easily than she did.

GLOSSARY OF BUSINESS TERMS USED IN THIS WORKBOOK

1:1 Meeting (One-on-One): A recurring, focused meeting between a lead and a team member to align on priorities, unblock work, and support development.

2-Minute Rule: A prioritisation tactic: if a task takes two minutes or less, do it immediately to reduce mental overhead and task switching.

360-Degree Feedback: A structured process gathering performance feedback from a lead, peers, and direct reports to provide a full-circle view of behaviours and impact.

70% Rule (Delegation): A guideline to delegate when someone can do a task at 70% of your current proficiency—and support them to grow beyond it.

ABCDE Method: A prioritisation framework that labels tasks A–E by importance and urgency to focus attention where it matters most.

Accountability Plan: A written agreement that clarifies commitments, owners, timelines, and follow-ups to ensure progress is tracked and delivered.

Active Listening: A communication skill that involves attention, reflection, and clarifying questions to fully understand the speaker's message.

Agenda: A planned list of topics, goals, and timings that sets expectations and keeps a meeting on track.

Alignment: Shared understanding of goals, priorities, and success measures across individuals or teams.

Annual Recurring Revenue (ARR): The total value of subscription revenue normalised to a one-year period.

Average Revenue per User (ARPU): The average revenue generated per customer over a defined period.

Boundaries: Agreed limits around time, availability, and responsibilities that protect focus and well-being.

Bottleneck: A constraint that slows or blocks throughput in a process or project.

Brainstorming: A divergent thinking activity to generate ideas without immediate judgement, often preceding selection and planning.

Brag Document: A running record of wins, impact, and feedback that supports confidence, reviews, and promotion cases.

Budget: A plan for allocating financial and human resources toward goals within given constraints.

Burnout: A state of emotional, mental, and physical exhaustion caused by chronic stress, often signalled by cynicism and reduced effectiveness.

CAC (Customer Acquisition Cost): The total sales and marketing spend required to acquire a new customer.

Candidate Profile: A concise description of the skills, behaviours, and values sought for a role to guide sourcing and interviews.

Career Growth: Progress in responsibilities, skills, scope, and impact over time.

Celebrating Wins: A practice of recognising progress and outcomes to reinforce effective behaviours and boost morale.

Check-In: A brief touchpoint (async or live) to surface status, blockers, and next steps.

Churn Rate: The percentage of customers or revenue lost over a period.

Coaching: A partnership that uses questions, reflection, and accountability to help someone clarify goals and take effective action.

Collaboration (Cross-Department): Working across teams and functions to achieve shared outcomes.

CSAT (Customer Satisfaction Score): A post-interaction rating (often 1–5) that reflects customer satisfaction.

CLV / LTV (Customer Lifetime Value): The net revenue expected from a customer over the entire relationship.

CRM (Customer Relationship Management): Systems and practices for tracking interactions, opportunities, and customer data.

Cultural Fit: The degree to which a candidate's behaviours and values align with the organisation and team.

Deep Work: Focused, uninterrupted effort on cognitively demanding tasks.

Delegation: Assigning responsibility and authority for tasks or outcomes, with clarity on ownership and support.

Deliverable: A tangible output or milestone promised by a specific date and owner.

Deadline: The agreed date or time by which a deliverable must be completed.

Do Not Disturb (DND): A settings mode that suppresses notifications to protect focus or rest.

"Do You Really Need That Meeting?" Framework: A decision aid for replacing unnecessary meetings with asynchronous updates or shorter formats.

EBITDA: Earnings before interest, taxes, depreciation, and amortisation; a proxy for operating profitability.

eNPS (Employee Net Promoter Score): An internal metric that gauges how likely employees are to recommend their workplace.

Eisenhower Matrix: A 2×2 prioritisation model that sorts tasks by urgency and importance.

Emotional Resilience: The capacity to recover from setbacks and sustain effective performance.

Empathy: The ability to understand and share another person's perspective and emotions.

Energy Management: Intentional planning of tasks and routines to match work demands with personal energy peaks.

Engagement: The degree of commitment, enthusiasm, and discretionary effort employees put into their work.

Focus Apps: Tools that reduce distractions (e.g., site blocking, soundscapes) to maintain concentration.

Feedback (Constructive): Specific, behaviour-based information intended to reinforce strengths or course-correct.

Gantt Chart: A timeline view that maps tasks, durations, dependencies, and progress for a project.

Goal (SMART): An objective designed to be Specific, Measurable, Achievable, Relevant, and Time-bound.

GROW Model: A coaching structure with stages: Goal, Reality, Options, and Way Forward.

Gross Margin: Revenue minus cost of goods or services, expressed as a percentage.

Growth and Development: Ongoing learning, upskilling, and expanded scope that increase a person's contribution and satisfaction.

Hallucinations (AI): Confident but incorrect outputs from an AI system, requiring human verification.

Hiring: The set of activities to attract, assess, and select candidates for open roles.

Ivy Lee Method: A daily planning routine of listing six priority tasks for the next day in order of importance.

Journaling: Writing to reflect on experiences, insights, and actions to reinforce learning and clarity.

KPI (Key Performance Indicator): A measurable indicator that tracks progress toward a goal.

Learning to Say No: Setting clear limits on scope or timing to protect priorities and well-being.

LLM (Large Language Model): A class of AI systems that generate or summarise text; useful for drafts and analysis when reviewed by humans.

Mentor: An experienced colleague who accelerates onboarding and growth through guidance and context.

Mind Mapping: A visual technique for organising ideas around a central concept to reveal relationships and options.

Motivational Interviewing: A coaching approach that strengthens a person's own motivation and commitment to change.

Monthly Recurring Revenue (MRR): Predictable subscription revenue recognised each month.

Net Promoter Score (NPS): A measure of customer loyalty based on recommendation likelihood.

Note-Taking: Capturing key decisions, actions, and learnings so information is retained and shared.

Objectives and Key Results (OKRs): A goal-setting system pairing an aspirational objective with measurable results.

Onboarding: A structured process that integrates new hires into the team, tools, and culture.

Operational Excellence: Systematic improvement of processes to increase quality, speed, and efficiency.

Options (GROW): The exploration of alternative strategies or paths to reach a goal.

Out-of-Office (OOO) Auto-Reply: An automatic message that sets response expectations during leave or deep-work periods.

Owner: The person accountable for delivering a task or outcome.

Pareto Principle (80/20 Rule): The observation that a vital few inputs drive the majority of results.

Performance Feedback (in 1:1s): Regular, specific guidance to reinforce strengths and address gaps.

Post-Mortem: A structured review after a project or incident to capture lessons and prevent repeat issues.

Prioritisation: The act of ranking work by impact and urgency to focus limited time and resources.

Privacy (AI Guardrail): The practice of removing sensitive data before using external tools.

Productivity: The effectiveness of converting time and effort into valuable outcomes.

Project Roadmap: A high-level sequence of milestones and releases that communicates direction and timing.

RACI Matrix: A responsibility chart that clarifies who is Responsible, Accountable, Consulted, and Informed.

Reality (GROW): The current state—facts, constraints, and resources—relative to the goal.

Reflection Exercise: A guided prompt set that helps capture insights, decisions, and next actions.

Resource Allocation: Assigning people, time, and budget to the most valuable work.

Employee Retention: The rate at which employees stay with the organisation over time.

Return on Investment (ROI): The gain from an investment relative to its cost, expressed as a percentage.

Risk Management: Identifying, assessing, and mitigating uncertainties that could impact outcomes.

Roadblocks (Blockers): Issues that prevent progress until resolved.

Sales Pipeline: A structured view of opportunities moving from lead to close.

Scheduling Tools: Applications that automate meeting coordination by exposing availability and options.

Shadowing: Short-term observation of an experienced colleague to learn tasks and context.

SMART Goals: See Goal (SMART); the five-part criteria that make goals clear and trackable.

Stakeholder: Any person or group with an interest in, or influence over, an outcome.

Stand-Up / Sitdown: Short, regular meetings used to report progress, surface blockers, and coordinate next steps.

Strategic Contribution: Work that advances long-term objectives beyond day-to-day execution.

CliftonStrengths: A strengths-based assessment used to identify and leverage natural talents.

Support Plan: A targeted set of actions, resources, and check-ins to help someone succeed in a new task or role.

SWOT Analysis: A framework to explore Strengths, Weaknesses, Opportunities, and Threats.

Team Morale: The collective confidence and enthusiasm within a team.

Team Performance: The degree to which a team meets or exceeds goals, deadlines, and quality standards.

Tech Tools for Productivity: Digital applications that streamline planning, collaboration, and execution.

Termination (Letting Someone Go): The process of ending employment while maintaining fairness, clarity, and dignity.

Time Blocking: Scheduling specific blocks of uninterrupted time for priority work.

Turnover Rate: The proportion of employees who leave during a given period.

Upskilling: Building new skills to increase effectiveness and future opportunities.

Values Assessment: A reflective process to clarify personal or team values that guide decisions and behaviour.

Way Forward (GROW): The specific actions, owners, and timelines chosen to move toward the goal.

Well-Being: Practices that sustain health, focus, and motivation over time.

Wheel of Life: A visual self-assessment that maps satisfaction across key life areas to identify imbalance and focus areas.

Work-In-Progress (WIP): A draft or partially complete output shared early to gather feedback and accelerate learning.

REFERENCES

Allen, D. (2015). *Getting things done: The art of stress-free productivity* (Rev. ed.). Penguin Books.

Asana, Inc. (2012). *Asana* (web-based productivity software). San Francisco, CA: Asana, Inc.

Atlassian. (2011). *Trello* (project management software). Sydney, Australia: Atlassian.

Bailey, C. (2018). *Hyperfocus: How to be more productive in a world of distraction*. Pan Macmillan.

Baumeister, R. F., & Tierney, J. (2011). *Willpower: Rediscovering the greatest human strength*. The Penguin Press.

Beyer, B., Jones, C., Petoff, J., & Murphy, N. R. (Eds.). (2016). *Site reliability engineering: How Google runs production systems*. O'Reilly Media.

Buckingham, M., & Clifton, D. O. (2001). *Now, discover your strengths*. New York, NY: Free Press.

Bungay Stanier, M. (2016). *The coaching habit: Say less, ask more & change the way you lead forever*. Post Hypnotic Press Incorporated.

Buzan, T., & Buzan, B. (1996). *The mind map book: How to use radiant thinking to maximize your brain's untapped potential*. Plume.

Calendly, LLC. (2013). *Calendly* [Computer software]. https://calendly.com

Carse, J. P. (2013). *Finite and infinite games: A vision of life as play and possibility*. Free Press.

ClickUp, Inc. (n.d.). *ClickUp* [Computer software]. https://clickup.com

Clear, J. (2016, October 3). *The Ivy Lee method: The daily routine experts recommend for peak productivity*. Retrieved from JamesClear.com: https://jamesclear.com/ivy-lee

Clegg, D., & Barker, R. (1994). *Case method fast-track: A RAD approach*. Reading, MA: Addison-Wesley.

ClydeBank Business. (2015). *Agile project management & Scrum: QuickStart guides*. ClydeBank Media LLC.

Covey, S. R. (2020). *The 7 habits of highly effective people*. Simon & Schuster.

Covey, S. R., Merrill, A. R., & Merrill, R. R. (1996). *First things first*. Simon & Schuster.

Csikszentmihalyi, M. (2008). *Flow: The psychology of optimal experience*. Harper & Collins.

Dicks, M. (2018). *Storyworthy: Engage, teach, persuade, and change your life through the power of storytelling*(Foreword by D. Kennedy). New World Library.

Doodle AG. (2007). *Doodle* [Computer software]. https://doodle.com

Doerr, J. (2018). *Measure what matters: How Google, Bono, and the Gates Foundation rock the world with OKRs*. New York, NY: Portfolio.

Doran, G. T. (1981). There's a S.M.A.R.T. way to write management's goals and objectives. *Management Review, 70*(11), 35–36.

Dropbox, Inc. (2008). *Dropbox* (file hosting service) [Computer software]. San Francisco, CA: Dropbox, Inc.

Dweck, C. S. (2006). *Mindset: The new psychology of success*. New York, NY: Random House.

Edmondson, A. (1999). Psychological safety and learning behavior in work teams. *Administrative Science Quarterly, 44*(2), 350–383. https://doi.org/10.2307/2666999

Edmondson, A. C. (2019). *The fearless organization: Creating psychological safety in the workplace for learning, innovation, and growth*. Hoboken, NJ: Wiley.

Edmondson, A. C. (2023). *Right kind of wrong: The science of failing well*. Atria Books.

Epstein, D. (2019). *Range: Why generalists triumph in a specialized world*. Riverhead Books.

Evans, J. (2019). Get your work recognized: Write a brag document. *jvns.ca*. https://jvns.ca/blog/brag-documents/

Evernote Corporation. (n.d.). *Evernote* [Computer software]. https://evernote.com

Fiore, N. (2007). *The now habit: A strategic program for overcoming procrastination and enjoying guilt-free play* (Rev. ed.). Tarcher.

Forte, T. (2022). *Building a second brain: A proven method to organize your digital life and unlock your creative potential.* Atria Books.

Forte, T. (2023). *The PARA method: Simplify, organize, and master your digital life.* Atria Books.

Frankl, V. E. (2006). *Man's search for meaning.* Beacon Press. (Original work published 1959)

Freedom Labs, Inc. (n.d.). *Freedom* [Computer software]. https://freedom.to

Fournier, C. (2017). *The manager's path: A guide for tech leaders navigating growth & change.* O'Reilly Media.

Goleman, D. (1995). *Emotional intelligence: Why it can matter more than IQ.* New York, NY: Bantam Books.

Goleman, D. (2000). Leadership that gets results. *Harvard Business Review, 78*(2), 78–90.

Google LLC. (2006). *Google Calendar* (calendar and scheduling tool) [Computer software]. Mountain View, CA: Google.

Google LLC. (2012). *Google Drive* (cloud storage service) [Computer software]. Mountain View, CA: Google.

Glasser, W. (1998). *Choice theory: A new psychology of personal freedom.* HarperCollins.

Grove, A. S. (1995). *High output management.* Vintage.

Gunaratana, B. H. (2011). *Mindfulness in plain English* (20th anniversary ed.). Wisdom Publications. (Original work published 1992)

Harvest. (n.d.). *Harvest* [Computer software]. https://www.getharvest.com

Hersey, P., & Blanchard, K. H. (1977). *Management of organizational behavior* (3rd ed.). Englewood Cliffs, NJ: Prentice Hall.

HubSpot, Inc. (n.d.). *HubSpot* [Computer software]. https://hubspot.com

Humphrey, A. S. (2005). SWOT analysis for management consulting. *SRI Alumni Newsletter. (Originator of SWOT technique at SRI, 1960s).*

Hyatt, M. (2019). *Free to focus: A total productivity system to achieve more by doing less.* Baker Books.

IFTTT, Inc. (2010). *IFTTT* [Computer software]. https://ifttt.com

International Coach Federation. (2019). *Core competencies.*

International Coach Federation. Retrieved from https://coachfederation.org/core-competencies

Johnson, E. J. (2021). *The elements of choice: Why the way we decide matters*. Riverhead Books.

Juhtimisest. (n.d.). *Liitev klass, liitev kool.* Retrieved October 8, 2025, from https://sisu.ut.ee/liitevklassliitevkool/juhtimisest/

Kahneman, D. (2011). *Thinking, fast and slow*. Farrar, Straus and Giroux.

Kaplan, R. S., & Norton, D. P. (1992). The balanced scorecard—Measures that drive performance. *Harvard Business Review, 70*(1), 71–79.

Kegan, R. (1994). *In over our heads: The mental demands of modern life*. Cambridge, MA: Harvard University Press.

Koch, R. (1998). *The 80/20 principle: The secret to achieving more with less*. New York, NY: Doubleday.

Kotter, J. P., & Rathgeber, H. (2006). *Our iceberg is melting: Changing and succeeding under any conditions*. St. Martin's Press.

Lepsinger, R., & Lucia, A. D. (1997). *The art and science of 360-degree feedback*. San Francisco, CA: Pfeiffer.

Levitin, D. J. (2014). *The organized mind: Thinking straight in the age of information overload*. Dutton.

Lieberman, D. J. (2022). *Mindreader: The new science of deciphering what people really think, what they really want, and who they really are*. St. Martin's Essentials.

Liker, J. K. (2004). *The Toyota way: 14 management principles from the world's greatest manufacturer.* McGraw-Hill.

Lunney, J., & Lueder, S. (2016). Postmortem culture: Learning from failure. In B. Beyer, C. Jones, J. Petoff, & N. R. Murphy (Eds.), *Site reliability engineering: How Google runs production systems*. O'Reilly Media. https://sre.google/sre-book/postmortem-culture/

Maltz, M. (2015). *Psycho-Cybernetics: Updated and expanded*. TarcherPerigee. (Original work published 1960)

Maslach, C., & Leiter, M. P. (1997). *The truth about burnout*. Jossey-Bass.

McBer and Company (1980). Trainer's Guide. Boston, McBer and Company. (p. 70).

McCarthy, B. (1981). *The 4MAT system: Teaching to learning styles with right/left mode techniques* (2nd rev. ed.). EXCEL, Inc.

McCord, P. (2018). *Powerful: Building a culture of freedom and responsibility*. Silicon Guild.

McKeown, G. (2014). *Essentialism: The disciplined pursuit of less*. New York, NY: Crown Business.

Meadows, D. H. (2008). *Thinking in systems: A primer*. White River Junction, VT: Chelsea Green.

MeisterLabs. (n.d.). *MindMeister* [Computer software]. https://www.mindmeister.com

Microsoft Corporation. (2014). *OneDrive* (cloud storage platform) [Computer software]. Redmond, WA: Microsoft.

Microsoft Corporation. (2003). *OneNote* [Computer software]. https://www.microsoft.com/microsoft-365/onenote

Microsoft Corporation. (2017). *Microsoft Teams* (collaboration software) [Computer software]. Redmond, WA: Microsoft.

Miller, W. R., & Rollnick, S. (2013). *Motivational interviewing: Helping people change* (3rd ed.). New York, NY: Guilford Press.

Monday.com Ltd. (n.d.). *monday.com* [Computer software]. https://monday.com

Newport, C. (2016). *Deep work: Rules for focused success in a distracted world*. Grand Central.

Notion Labs, Inc. (2016). *Notion* (productivity software) [Computer software]. San Francisco, CA: Notion Labs.

Osborn, A. F. (1953). *Applied imagination: Principles and procedures of creative problem-solving*. New York, NY: Charles Scribner's Sons.

Paul, A. M. (2021). *The extended mind: The power of thinking outside the brain*. Houghton Mifflin Harcourt.

Pareto, V. (1896). *Cours d'économie politique* (Vols. 1–2). Lausanne, Switzerland: F. Rouge.

Parkinson, C. N. (1958). *Parkinson's law: The pursuit of progress*. London, UK: John Murray.

Petersen, A. H. (2019). *The burnout generation*. Amazon Original Stories.

Pinker, S. (2007). *The stuff of thought: Language as a window into human nature*. Viking.

Pressfield, S. (2002). *The war of art: Break through the blocks and win your inner creative battles*. Warner Books.

Pressfield, S. (2011). *Do the work*. Do You Zoom, Inc.

Project Management Institute. (2017). *A guide to the project management body of knowledge (PMBOK® Guide)* (6th ed.). Newtown Square, PA: PMI.

Rath, T. (2007). *StrengthsFinder 2.0*. New York, NY: Gallup Press.

Reichheld, F. F. (2003). The one number you need to grow. *Harvard Business Review, 81*(12), 46–54.

Robson, D. (2019). *The intelligence trap: Why smart people make dumb mistakes*. W. W. Norton & Company.

Rogers, C. R., & Farson, R. E. (1957). *Active listening*. Chicago, IL: Industrial Relations Center, University of Chicago.

Rosling, H., Rosling, O., & Rosling Rönnlund, A. (2018). *Factfulness: Ten reasons we're wrong about the world—and why things are better than you think*. Flatiron Books.

Salesforce, Inc. (n.d.). *Salesforce* [Computer software]. https://salesforce.com

Saunders, E. G. (2015, March 11). Do you really need to hold that meeting? *Harvard Business Review*. Retrieved from https://hbr.org/2015/03/do-you-really-need-to-hold-that-meeting

Scannell, E. E., & Newstrom, J. W. (1980). *Games trainers play: Experiential learning exercises*. New York, NY: McGraw-Hill.

Schein, E. H. (2010). *Organizational culture and leadership* (4th ed.). Jossey-Bass.

Schleckser, J. (2016). *Great CEOs are lazy: How exceptional CEOs do more in less time*. New York, NY: Inc. Original Imprint (Mansueto Ventures).

Schwarzenegger, A. (2023). *Be useful: Seven tools for life*. The Penguin Press.

Scott, K. (2017). *Radical candor: Be a kick-ass boss without losing your humanity*. St. Martin's Press.

Seekrtech Co., Ltd. (n.d.). *Forest* [Computer software]. https://www.forestapp.cc

Sinek, S. (2019). *The infinite game*. Portfolio/Penguin.

Slack Technologies. (2013). *Slack* (communication platform) [Computer software]. San Francisco, CA: Slack Technologies.

Smart, B. D. (2012). *Topgrading* (3rd ed.). Portfolio.

Smart, G., & Street, R. (2008). *Who: The A method for hiring.* Crown Business.

Stone, D., & Heen, S. (2014). *Thanks for the feedback: The science and art of receiving feedback well.* Viking.

Stroh, D. P. (2015). *Systems thinking for social change: A practical guide to solving complex problems, avoiding unintended consequences, and achieving lasting results.* Chelsea Green Publishing.

Swart, J. (2022). *The wheel of life as a coaching tool to audit life priorities.* ResearchGate. https://www.researchgate.net/publication/365375169_The_Wheel_of_Life_as_a_Coaching_Tool_to_Audit_Life_Priorities

Syed, M. (2015). *Black box thinking: Why most people never learn from their mistakes—but some do.* Portfolio.

Tawwab, N. G. (2021). *Set boundaries, find peace: A guide to reclaiming yourself.* TarcherPerigee.

Toggl OÜ. (n.d.). *Toggl Track* [Computer software]. https://toggl.com/track

Trimboli, O. (2022). *How to listen: Discover the hidden key to better communication.* Page Two Books.

Tracy, B. (2001). *Eat that frog!: 21 great ways to stop procrastinating and get more done in less time.* San Francisco, CA: Berrett-Koehler.

Voss, C., & Raz, T. (2016). *Never split the difference: Negotiating as if your life depended on it.* Harper Business.

Walker, M. (2017). *Why we sleep: Unlocking the power of sleep and dreams.* Scribner.

Watkins, M. D. (2013). *The first 90 days: Proven strategies for getting up to speed faster and smarter* (Updated ed.). Harvard Business Review Press.

Weitzel, S. R. (2019). *Feedback that works: How to build and deliver your message* (2nd ed.). Center for Creative Leadership.

Whitmore, J. (1992). *Coaching for performance: A practical guide to growing your own skills.* London, UK: Nicholas Brealey.

Whitworth, L., Kimsey-House, H., Kimsey-House, K., & Sandahl, P. (2018). *Co-Active coaching* (4th ed.). Nicholas Brealey.

Wolff, S. B. (2005, November). *Emotional competence inventory (ECI) technical manual* (Version 2.0). Hay Group, McClelland

Center for Research and Innovation. https://www.eiconsortium.org/pdf/ECI_2_0_Technical_Manual_v2.pdf

XMind Ltd. (n.d.). *XMind* [Computer software]. https://xmind.app

Young, S. H. (2019). *Ultralearning: Master hard skills, outsmart the competition, and accelerate your career*. Harper Business.

Zapier, Inc. (2011). *Zapier* [Computer software]. https://zapier.com